# The English

Jacques Casanova de Seingalt

[ZHINGOORA BOOKS]

# THE ENGLISH

## CHAPTER X

*Eccentricity of the English—Castelbajac Count Schwerin—Sophie at School—My Reception at the Betting Club—The Charpillon*

I passed a night which seemed like a never-ending nightmare, and I got up sad and savage, feeling as if I could kill a man on the smallest provocation. It seemed as if the house, which I had hitherto thought so beautiful, was like a millstone about my neck. I went out in my travelling clothes, and walked into a coffee-house, where I saw a score of people reading the papers.

I sat down, and, not understanding English, passed my time in gazing at the goers and comers. I had been there some time when my attention was attracted by the voice of a man speaking as follows in French:

"Tommy has committed suicide, and he was wise, for he was in such a state that he could only expect unhappiness for the rest of his life."

"You are quite mistaken," said the other, with the greatest composure. "I was one of his creditors myself, and on making an inventory of his effects I feel satisfied that he has done a very foolish and a very childish thing; he might have lived on comfortably, and not killed himself for fully six months."

At any other time this calculation would have made me laugh, and, as it was, I felt as if the incident had done me good.

I left the coffee-house without having said a word or spent a penny, and I went towards the Exchange to get some money. Bosanquet gave me what I wanted directly, and as I walked out with him I noticed a curious-looking individual, whose name I asked.

"He's worth a hundred thousand," said the banker.

"And who is that other man over there?"

"He's not worth a ten-pound note."

"But I don't want to hear what they are worth; it's their names I want."

"I really don't know."

"How can you tell how much they are worth, not knowing their names?"

"Names don't go for anything here. What we want to know about a man is how much he has got? Besides; what's in a name? Ask me for a thousand pounds and give me a proper receipt, and you can do it under the name of Socrates or Attila, for all I care. You will pay me back my money as Socrates or Attila, and not as Seingalt; that is all."

"But how about signing bills of exchange?"

"That's another thing; I must use the name which the drawer gives me."

"I don't understand that."

"Well, you see, you are not English, nor are you a business man."

On leaving him I walked towards the park, but wishing to change a twenty-pound note before going in I went to a fat merchant, an epicure whose acquaintance I had made at the tavern, and put down the note on his counter, begging him to cash it for me.

"Come again in an hour," said he, "I have no money by me just now."

"Very good; I will call again when I come from the park."

"Take back your note; you shall give it to me when I hand you the money."

"Never mind; keep it. I don't doubt your honesty."

"Don't be so foolish. If you left me the note I should certainly decline to hand over the money, if only for the sake of giving you a lesson."

"I don't believe you are capable of such dishonesty."

"Nor am I, but when it comes to such a simple thing as putting a bank note in your pocket, the most honest man in the world would never dream of having such a thing in his possession without having paid the money for it, and the least slip of memory might lead to a dispute in which you would infallibly come off second best."

"I feel the force of your arguments, especially in a town where so much business is carried on."

When I got into the park I met Martinelli and thanked him for sending me a copy of the Decameron, while he congratulated me on my re-appearance in society, and on the young lady of whom I had been the happy possessor and no doubt the slave.

"My Lord Pembroke has seen her," said he, "and thought her charming."

"What? Where could he have seen her?"

"In a carriage with you driving fast along the Rochester road. It is three or four days ago."

"Then I may tell you that I was taking her to Calais; I shall never see her face again."

"Will you let the room again in the same way?"

"No, never again, though the god of love has been propitious to me. I shall be glad to see you at my house whenever you like to come."

"Shall I send you a note to warn you?"

"Not at all."

We walked on talking about literature, manners, and so forth, in an aimless way. All at once, as we approached Buckingham House, I saw five or six persons, relieving nature amidst the bushes, with their hinder parts facing the passers-by. I thought this a disgusting piece of indecency, and said as much to Martinelli, adding that the impudent rascals might at least turn their faces towards the path.

"Not at all," he exclaimed, "for then they might be recognized; whereas in exposing their posteriors they run no such risk; besides the sight makes squeamish persons turn away."

"You are right, but you will confess that the whole thing strikes a stranger as very revolting."

"Yes, there is nothing so ineradicable as national prejudice. You may have noticed that when an Englishman wants to ease his sluices in the street, he doesn't run up an alley or turn to the wall like we do."

"Yes, I have noticed them turning towards the middle of the street, but if they thus escape the notice of the people in the shops and on the pavement they are seen by everybody who is driving in a carriage, and that is as bad."

"The people in the carriages need not look."

"That is true."

We walked on to the Green Park, and met Lord Pembroke on horseback. He stopped and burst into exclamations on seeing me. As I guessed the cause of his surprise, I hastened to tell him that I was a free man once more, to my sorrow, and felt lonely amidst my splendour.

"I feel rather curious about it, and perhaps I may come and keep you company to-day."

We parted, and reckoning on seeing him at dinner I, went back to tell my cook that dinner was to be served in the large room.

Martinelli had an engagement and could not come to dinner, but he led me out of the park by a door with which I was not acquainted, and sent me on my way.

As we were going along we saw a crowd of people who seemed to be staring at something. Martinelli went up to the crowd, and then returned to me, saying,—

"That's a curious sight for you; you can enter it amidst your remarks on English manners."

"What is it?"

"A man at the point of death from a blow he has received in boxing with another sturdy fellow."

"Cannot anything be done?"

"There is a surgeon there who would bleed him, if he were allowed."

"Who could prevent him?"

"That's the curious part of it. Two men have betted on his death or recovery. One says, 'I'll bet twenty guineas he dies,' and the other says, 'Done.' Number one will not allow the surgeon to bleed him, for if the man recovered his twenty guineas would be gone."

"Poor man! what pitiless betters!"

"The English are very strange in their betting proclivities; they bet about everything. There is a Betting Club to which I will introduce you, if you like."

"Do they speak French there?"

"Most certainly, for it is composed of men of wit and mark."

"What do they do?"

"They talk and argue, and if one man brings forward a proposition which another denies, and one backs his opinion, the other has to bet too, on pain of a fine which goes to the common fund."

"Introduce me to this delightful club, by all means; it will make my fortune, for I shall always take care to be on the right side."

"You had better be careful; they are wary birds."

"But to return to the dying man; what will be done to his antagonist?"

"His hand will be examined, and if it is found to be just the same as yours or mine it will be marked, and he will be let go."

"I don't understand that, so kindly explain. How do they recognize a dangerous hand?"

"If it is found to be marked already, it is a proof that he has killed his man before and has been marked for it, with the warning, 'Take care not to kill anyone else, for if you do you will be hanged.'"

"But supposing such a man is attacked?"

"He ought to shew his hand, and then his adversary would let him alone."

"But if not?"

"Then he is defending himself; and if he kills his man he is acquitted, provided he can bring witnesses to swear that he was obliged to fight."

"Since fighting with the fist may cause death, I wonder it is allowed."

"It is only allowed for a wager. If the combatants do not put one or more pieces of money on the ground before the fight, and there is a death, the man is hanged."

"What laws! What manners!"

In such ways I learnt much concerning the manner and customs of this proud nation, at once so great and so little.

The noble lord came to dinner, and I treated him in a manner to make him wish to come again. Although there were only the two of us, the meal lasted a long time, as I was anxious for additional information on what I had heard in the morning, especially on the Betting Club. The worthy Pembroke advised me not to have anything to do with it, unless I made up my mind to keep perfect silence for four or five weeks.

"But supposing they ask me a question?"

"Evade it."

"Certainly, if I am not in a position to give my opinion; but if I have an opinion, the powers of Satan could not shut my mouth."

"All the worse for you."

"Are the members knaves?"

"Certainly not. They are noblemen, philosophers, and epicures; but they are pitiless where a bet is concerned."

"Is the club treasury rich?"

"Far from it; they are all ashamed to pay a fine, and prefer to bet. Who will introduce you?"

"Martinelli."

"Quite so; through Lord Spencer, who is a member. I would not become one."

"Why not?"

"Because I don't like argument."

"My taste runs the other way, so I shall try to get in."

"By the way, M. de Seingalt, do you know that you are a very extraordinary man?"

"For what reason, my lord?"

"You shut yourself up for a whole month with a woman who spent fourteen months in London without anybody making her acquaintance or even discovering her nationality. All the amateurs have taken a lively interest in the affair."

"How did you find out that she spent fourteen months in London?"

"Because several persons saw her in the house of a worthy widow where she spent the first month. She would never have anything to say to any advances, but the bill in your window worked wonders."

"Yes, and all the worse for me, for I feel as if I could never love another woman."

"Oh, that's childish indeed! You will love another woman in a week-nay, perhaps to-morrow, if you will come and dine with me at my country house. A perfect French beauty has asked me to dine with her. I have told some of my friends who are fond of gaming."

"Does the charming Frenchwoman like gaming?"

"No, but her husband does."

"What's his name?"

"He calls himself Count de Castelbajac."

"Ah! Castelbajac?"

"Yes."

"He is a Gascon?"

"Yes."

"Tall, thin, and dark, and marked with the smallpox?

"Exactly! I am delighted to find you know him. You will agree with me that his wife is very pretty?"

"I really can't say. I knew Castelbajac, as he calls himself, six years ago, and I never heard he was married. I shall be delighted to join you, however. I must warn you not to say anything if he seems not to know me; he may possibly have good reasons for acting in that manner. Before long I will tell you a story which does not represent him in a very advantageous manner. I did not know he played. I shall take care to be on my guard at the Betting Club, and I advise you, my lord, to be on your guard in the society of Castelbajac."

"I will not forget the warning."

When Pembroke had left me I went to see Madame Cornelis, who had written a week before to tell me my daughter was ill, and explained that she had been turned from my doors on two occasions though she felt certain I was in. To this I replied that I was in love, and so happy within my own house that I had excluded all strangers, and with that she had to be contented, but the state in which I found little Sophie frightened me. She was lying in bed with high fever, she had grown much thinner, and her eyes seemed to say that she was dying of grief. Her mother was in despair, for she was passionately fond of the child, and I thought she would have torn my eyes out when I told her that if Sophie died she would only have herself to reproach. Sophie, who was very good-hearted, cried out, "No, no! papa dear;" and quieted her mother by her caresses.

Nevertheless, I took the mother aside, and told her that the disease was solely caused by Sophie's dread of her severity.

"In spite of your affection," said I, "you treat her with insufferable tyranny. Send her to a boarding-school for a couple of years, and let her associate with girls of good family. Tell her this evening that she is to go to school, and see if she does not get better."

"Yes," said she, "but a good boarding-school costs a hundred guineas a year, including masters."

"If I approve of the school you select I will pay a year in advance."

On my making this offer the woman, who seemed to be living so luxuriously, but was in reality poverty-stricken, embraced me with the utmost gratitude.

"Come and tell the news to your daughter now," said she, "I should like to watch her face when she hears it."

"Certainly."

"My dear Sophie," I said, "your mother agrees with me that if you had a change of air you would get better, and if you would like to spend a year or two in a good school I will pay the first year in advance."

"Of course, I will obey my dear mother," said Sophie.

"There is no question of obedience. Would you like to go to school? Tell me truly."

"But would my mother like me to go?"

"Yes, my child, if it would please you."

"Then, mamma, I should like to go very much."

Her face flushed as she spoke, and I knew that my diagnosis had been correct. I left her saying I should hope to hear from her soon.

At ten o'clock the next day Jarbe came to ask if I had forgotten my engagement.

"No," said I, "but it is only ten o'clock."

"Yes, but we have twenty miles to go."

"Twenty miles?"

"Certainly, the house is at St. Albans."

"It's very strange Pembroke never told me; how did you find out the address?"

"He left it when he went away:"

"Just like an Englishman."

I took a post-chaise, and in three hours I had reached my destination. The English roads are excellent, and the country offers a smiling prospect on every side. The vine is lacking, for though the English soil is fertile it will not bear grapes.

Lord Pembroke's house was not a particularly large one, but twenty masters and their servants could easily be accommodated in it.

The lady had not yet arrived, so my lord shewed me his gardens, his fountains, and his magnificent hot-houses; also a cock chained by the leg, and of a truly ferocious aspect.

"What have we here, my lord?"

"A cock."

"I see it is, but why do you chain it?"

"Because it is savage. It is very amorous, and if it were loose it would go after the hens, and kill all the cocks on the country-side."

"But why do you condemn him to celibacy?"

"To make him fiercer. Here, this is the list of his conquests."

He gave me a list of his cock's victories, in which he had killed the other bird; this had happened more than thirty times. He then shewed me the steel spurs, at the sight of which the cock began to ruffle and crow. I could not help laughing to see such a martial spirit in so small an animal. He seemed possessed by the demon of strife, and lifted now one foot and now the other, as if to beg that his arms might be put on.

Pembroke then exhibited the helmet, also of steel.

"But with such arms," said I, "he is sure of conquest."

"No; for when he is armed cap-a-pie he will not fight with a defenceless cock."

"I can't believe it, my lord."

"It's a well-known fact. Here, read this."

He then gave me a piece of paper with this remarkable biped's pedigree. He could prove his thirty-two quarters more easily than a good many noblemen, on the father's side, be it understood, for if he could have proved pure blood on the mother's side as well, Lord Pembroke would have decorated him with the Order of the Golden Fleece at least.

"The bird cost me a hundred guineas," said he, "but I would not sell him for a thousand."

"Has he any offspring?"

"He tries his best, but there are difficulties."

I do not remember whether Lord Pembroke explained what these difficulties were. Certainly the English offer more peculiarities to the attentive observer than any other nation.

At last a carriage containing a lady and two gentlemen drove up to the door. One of the gentlemen was the rascally Castelbajac and the other was introduced as Count Schwerin, nephew of the famous marshal of that name who fell on what is commonly called the field of glory. General Bekw—— an Englishman who was in the service of the King of Prussia, and was one of Pembroke's guests, received Schwerin politely, saying that he had seen his uncle die; at this the modest nephew drew the Order of the Black Eagle from his breast, and shewed it to us all covered with blood.

"My uncle wore it on the day of his death, and the King of Prussia allowed me to keep it as a noble memorial of my kinsman."

"Yes," said an Englishman who was present, "but the coat-pocket is not the place for a thing like that."

Schwerin made as if he did not understand, and this enabled me to take his measure.

Lord Pembroke took possession of the lady, whom I did not think worthy of being compared to Pauline. She was paler and shorter, and utterly deficient in Pauline's noble air; besides, when she smiled it spoiled her face, and this is a defect in a woman, to whom laughter should always be becoming.

Lord Pembroke introduced us all to each other, and when he came to me Castelbajac said he was delighted to see me again, although he might easily have pretended not to know me under my name of Seingalt.

We had a good English dinner, and afterwards the lady proposed a game of faro. My lord never played, so the general consented to amuse the company by holding the bank, and placed a hundred guineas and several bank notes on the table. There might be a thousand guineas in all. He then gave twenty counters to each punter, saying that every counter was worth ten shillings. As I only staked gold against gold I would not accept them. By the third deal Schwerin had lost his twenty counters and asked for twenty more; but the banker told him he must pay for them, and the self-styled field-marshal's nephew lapsed into silence and played no more.

At the following deal Castelbajac was in the same position as his friend, and being on my side he begged to be allowed to take ten pieces.

"You will bring me ill-luck," I said, coldly, warding off his hand; and he went out to the garden, no doubt to swallow the affront he had received. The lady said her husband had forgotten his pocketbook. An hour afterwards the game came to an end, and I took my leave, after inviting Lord Pembroke and the rest of the company to dine with me the next day.

I got home at eleven o'clock without meeting any highwaymen as I had expected, indeed I had put up six guineas in a small purse for their special use and benefit. I woke up my cook to tell him that the next day I should have twelve people to dinner, and that I hoped he would do me honour. I found a letter from Madame Cornelis on my table telling me that she and her daughter would drive with me on the following Sunday, and that we could go and see the boarding-school she had selected.

Next day Lord Pembroke and the fair Frenchwoman were the first to arrive. They drove in a carriage with two rather uncomfortable seats, but this discomfort is favourable to love. The Gascon and the Prussian were the last to come.

We sat down to table at two and left it at four, all of us well pleased with the cook, and still more so with the wine merchant; for though we had emptied forty bottles of wine, not one of us was at all intoxicated.

After coffee had been served the general invited us all to sup with him, and Madame Castelbajac begged me to hold a bank. I did not wait to be pressed but placed a thousand guineas on the table, and as I had no counters of any kind I warned the company that I would only play gold against gold, and that I should stop playing whenever I thought fit.

Before the game began the two counts paid their losses of the day before to the general in bank notes, which he begged me to change. I also changed two other notes presented to me by the same gentleman, and put them all under my snuff-box. Play began. I had no croupier, so I was obliged to deal slowly and keep an eye on the two counts, whose method of play was very questionable. At last both of them were dried up, and Castelbajac gave me a bill of exchange for two hundred guineas, begging me to discount it for him.

"I know nothing about business," I replied.

An Englishman took the bill, and after a careful examination said he neither knew the drawer, the accepter, nor the backer.

"I am the backer," said Castelbajac, "and that ought to be enough, I think."

Everybody laughed, besides myself, and I gave it him back courteously, saying politely that he could get it discounted on 'Change the next day. He got up in a bad temper, and left the room, murmuring some insolent expressions. Schwering followed him.

After these two worthy gentlemen had left us, I went on dealing till the night was far advanced, and then left off, though I was at a loss. However, the general had a run of luck, and I thought it best to stop. Before leaving he took me and Lord Pembroke aside, and begged me to contrive that the two knaves should not come to his house the following day. "For," said he, "if that Gascon were to be half as insolent to me as he was to you, I should shew him out by the window."

Pembroke said he would tell the lady of the general's wishes.

"Do you think," said I, "that those four notes of theirs can be forgeries?"

"It's very possible."

"What would you advise my doing to clear the matter up?"

"I would send them to the bank."

"And if they should be forgeries?"

"I would have patience, or I would arrest the rascals."

The next day I went to the bank myself, and the person to whom I gave the notes gave me them back, saying, coldly,—

"These notes are bad, sir."

"Be kind enough to examine them closely."

"It's no good, they are evident forgeries. Return them to the person from whom you got them, and he will be only too glad to cash them."

I was perfectly aware that I could put the two knaves under lock and key, but I did not want to do so. I went to Lord Pembroke to find out their address, but he was still in bed, and one of his servants took me to them. They were surprised to see me. I told them coolly enough that the four notes were forged, and that I should feel much obliged if they would give me forty guineas and take their notes back.

"I haven't got any money," said Castelbajac, "and what you say astonishes me very much. I can only return them to the persons who gave them to me, if the are really the same notes that we gave you yesterday."

At this suggestion the blood rushed to my face, and with a withering glance and an indignant apostrophe I left them. Lord Pembroke's servant took me to a magistrate who, having heard my statement on oath, gave me a paper authorizing me to arrest two counts. I gave the document to an alderman, who said he would see it was carried out, and I went home ill pleased with the whole business.

Martinelli was waiting for me; he had come to ask me to give him a dinner. I told him my story, without adding that the knaves were to be arrested, and his advice delivered with philosophic calm was to make an auto-da-fe of the four notes. It was very good advice, but I did not take it.

The worthy Martinelli, thinking to oblige me, told me that he had arranged with Lord Spencer the day on which I was to be introduced to the club, but I answered that my fancy for going there was over. I ought to have treated this learned and distinguished man with more politeness, but who can sound human weakness to its depths? One often goes to a wise man for advice which one has not the courage to follow.

In the evening I went to the general's, and found the self-styled Countess Castelbajac seated on Lord Pembroke's knees. The supper was a good one, and passed off pleasantly; the two rascals were not there, and their absence was not remarked. When we left the table we went into another room, and played till day-break. I left the board with a loss of two or three hundred guineas.

I did not wake till late the next morning, and when I did my man told me that a person wanted to speak to me. I had him shewn in, and as he only spoke English the negro had to be our interpreter. He was the chief of the police, and told me that if I would pay for the journey he would arrest Castelbajac at Dover, for which town he had started at noon. As to the other he was sure of having him in the course of the night. I gave him a guinea, and told him it would be enough to catch the one, and that the other could go where he liked.

The next day was Sunday, the only day on which Madame Cornelis could go abroad without fear of the bailiff. She came to dine with me, and brought her daughter, whom the prospect of leaving her mother had quite cured. The school which Madame Cornelis had chosen was at Harwich, and we went there after dinner.

The head-mistress was a Catholic, and though she must have been sixty, she looked keen, witty, and as if she knew the ways of the world. She had received an introduction from Lady Harrington, and so welcomed the young lady in the most cordial manner. She had about fifteen young boarders of thirteen or fourteen years of age. When she presented Sophie to them as a new companion, they crowded round her and covered her with caresses. Five or six were perfect angels of beauty, and two or three were hideously ugly; and such extremes are more common in England than anywhere else. My daughter was the smallest of them all, but as far as beauty went she had nothing to fear by comparison, and her talents placed her on a par with the eldest, while she responded to their caresses with that ease which later in life is only acquired with great difficulty.

We went over the house, and all the girls followed us, and those who could speak French or Italian spoke to me, saying how much they would love my daughter, while those who could not speak sufficiently well held off as if ashamed of their ignorance. We saw the bedrooms, the dining-room, the drawing-room, the harps and the pianos—in fact, everything, and I decided that Sophie could not be better placid. We went into the head-mistress's private room, and Madame Cornelis paid her a hundred guineas in advance, and obtained a receipt. We then agreed that Sophie should be received as a boarder as soon as she liked to come, that she was to bring her bed with her, and all the necessary linen. Madame Cornelis made the final arrangements on the ensuing Sunday.

Next day the alderman told me that Count Schwerin was a prisoner, and wanted to speak to me. I declined at first, but as the alderman's messenger told me, through Jarbe, that the poor devil had not a farthing in his pocket, I was moved with compassion. As he was charged with uttering forged notes he had been taken to Newgate, and was in danger of being hanged.

I followed the magistrate's messenger, and cannot say how the woeful aspect, the tears and supplications for mercy of the poor wretch, moved my heart. He swore that Castelbajac had given him the notes, but he added that he knew where they came from originally, and would tell me if I would release him.

A little bitterness still remained in my breast, so I told him that if he knew who forged the notes he could certainly escape the gallows, but that I should keep him prisoner till I got my money back. At this threat his tears and supplications began over again and with renewed force, and telling me that he was in utter poverty he emptied his pockets one after the other to shew me that he had no money, and at last offered me the bloodstained badge of his uncle. I was delighted to be able to relieve him without any appearance of weakness, and accepted the bauble as a pledge, telling him that he should have it back on payment of forty pounds.

I wrote out a formal release, and in his presence and in that of the alderman I burnt the four notes and set him free.

Two days afterwards the so-called countess came to my house, saying that now Castelbajac and Schewirin were gone, she knew not where to lay her head. She complained bitterly of Lord Pembroke, who deserted her after making her give him the clearest proofs of her affection. By way of consolation I told her that it would be very foolish of him to have abandoned her before instead of after.

To get rid of her I was obliged to give her the money to pay her journey to Calais. She told me she did not want to rejoin the Gascon, who was not really her husband. We shall hear more of these persons in the course of three years.

Two or three days later an Italian called on me, and gave me a letter from my friend Baletti, which recommended the bearer, Constantini, a native of Vicenza, to my good offices. He had come to London on a matter of importance in which I could help him.

I assured M. Constantini that I was only too happy to do anything to justify the confidence placed in my by one of my best friends, and he said that the long journey had almost exhausted his purse; but he added,—

"I know that my wife lives here, and that she is rich. I shall easily find out where she lives, and you know that as I am her husband all that is hers is mine."

"I was not aware of that."

"Then you don't know the laws of this country?"

"Not at all."

"I am sorry to hear it, but such is the case. I am going to her house, and I shall turn her out of doors with nothing else than the dress on her back, for the furniture, clothes, jewels, linen-in fact, all her possessions, belong to me. May I ask you to be with me when I perform this exploit?"

I was astonished. I asked him if he had told Baletti what he intended to do.

"You are the first person to whom I have disclosed my intentions."

I could not treat him as a madman, for he did not look like one, and, concluding that there really might be the law he had alleged, I replied that I did not feel inclined to join him in his enterprise, of which I disapproved very strongly, unless his wife had actually robbed him of what she possessed.

"She has only robbed me of my honour, sir, and she left me, taking her talents with her. She must have made a great fortune here, and have I not a right to take it from her, were it only for vengeance sake?"

"That may be, but I ask you what you would think of me if I agreed to join you in an undertaking which seems a cruel one to me, however good your reasons may be. Besides I may know your wife, she may even be a friend of mine."

"I will tell you her name."

"No, I beg of you not to do so, although I do not know any Madame

Constantini."

"She has changed her name to Calori, and she sings at the 'Haymarket.'"

"I know who she is now. I am sorry you have told me."

"I have no doubt you will keep my secret, and I am now going to find out where she lives; for that is the principal thing."

He left me weeping, and I pitied him, but at the same time I was sorry that he had made me the depositary of his secret. A few hours after I called on Madame Binetti, and she told me the histories of all the artistes in London. When she came to the Calori she told me that she had had several lovers out of whom she had made a great deal, but at present she had no lover, unless it were the violinist Giardini, with whom she was in love in earnest.

"Where does she come from?"

"From Vicenza."

"Is she married?"

"I don't think so."

I thought no more of this wretched business, but three or four days later I had a letter from King's Bench Prison. It was from Constantini. The poor wretch said I was the only friend he had in

London, and that he hoped I would come and see him, were it only to give him some advice.

I thought it my duty to accede to his request, and I went to the prison, where I found the poor man in a wretched state, with an old English attorney, who spoke a little bad Italian, and was known to me.

Constantini had been arrested the day before on account of several bills drawn by his wife which had not been taken up. By these bills she appeared in debt to the amount of a thousand guineas. The attorney had got the five bills, and he was trying to make some arrangements with the husband.

I saw at once that the whole thing was a scandalous swindle, for Madame Binetti had told me that the Calori was very rich. I begged the attorney to leave me alone with the prisoner, as I wanted to have some private conversation with him.

"They have arrested me for my wife's debts," said he, "and they tell me I must pay them because I am her husband."

"It's a trick your wife has played on you; she must have found out you were in London."

"She saw me through the window."

"Why did you delay putting your project into execution?"

"I meant to carry it out this morning, but how was I to know that she had debts?"

"Nor has she any debts; these bills are shams. They must have been ante-dated, for they were really executed yesterday. It's a bad business, and she may have to pay dearly for it."

"But in the meanwhile I am in prison."

"Never mind, trust to me, I will see you again tomorrow."

This scurvy trick had made me angry, and I made up my mind to take up the poor man's cause. I went to Bosanquet, who told me that the device was a very common one in London, but that people had found out the way to defeat it. Finally, he said that if the prisoner interested me he would put the case into the hands of a barrister who would extricate him from his difficulty, and make the wife and the lover, who had probably helped her, repent of their day's work. I begged him to act as if my interests were at stake, and promised to guarantee all expenses.

"That's enough," said he; "don't trouble yourself any more about it."

Same days after Mr. Bosanquet came to tell me that Constantini had left the prison and England as well, according to what the barrister who had charge of the case told him.

"Impossible!"

"Not at all. The lover of his wife, foreseeing the storm that was about to burst over their heads, got round the fellow, and made him leave the country by means of a sum more or less large."

The affair was over, but it was soon in all the newspapers, garnished with all the wit imaginable, and Giardini was warmly praised for the action he had taken.

As for me I was glad enough to have the matter over, but I felt vexed with Constantini for having fled without giving the lovers a lesson. I wrote an account of the circumstances to Baletti, and I heard from Madame Binetti that the Calori had given her husband a hundred guineas to leave the country. Some years later I saw the Calori at Prague.

A Flemish officer, the man whom I had helped at Aix-la-Chapelle, had called on me several times, and had even dined three or four times with me. I reproached myself for not having been polite enough to return his call, and when we met in the street, and he reproached me for not having been to see him, I was obliged to blush. He had his wife and daughter with him, and some feeling of shame and a good deal of curiosity made me call on him.

When he saw me he threw his arms about my neck, calling me his preserver. I was obliged to receive all the compliments which knaves make to honest men when they hope to take them in. A few moments after, an old woman and a girl came in, and I was introduced as the Chevalier de Seingalt, of whom he had spoken so often. The girl, affecting surprise, said she had known a M. Casanova, who was very like me. I answered that Casanova was my name as well as Seingalt, but that I had not the happiness of recollecting her.

"My name was Anspergher when I saw you," she replied, "but now it is Charpillon; and considering that we only met once, and that I was only thirteen at the time, I do not wonder at your not recollecting me. I have been in London with my mother and aunts for the last four years."

"But where had I the pleasure of speaking to you?"

"At Paris."

"In what part of Paris?"

"In the Bazaar. You were with a charming lady, and you gave me these buckles" (she shewed me them on her shoes), "and you also did me the honour to kiss me."

I recollected the circumstance, and the reader will remember that I was with Madame Baret, the fair stocking-seller.

"Now I remember you," said I; "but I do not recognize your aunt."

"This is the sister of the one you saw, but if you will take tea with us you will see her."

"Where do you live?"

"In Denmark Street, Soho."

## CHAPTER XI

The Charpillon—Dreadful Consequences of My Acquaintance With Her

The name Charpillon reminded me that I was the bearer of a letter for her, and drawing it from my pocket-book I gave it her, saying that the document ought to cement our acquaintance.

"What!" she exclaimed, "a letter from the dear ambassador Morosini. How delighted I am to have it! And you have actually been all these months in London without giving it me?"

"I confess I am to blame, but, as you see, the note has no address on it. I am grateful for the chance which has enabled me to discharge my commission to-day."

"Come and dine with us to-morrow."

"I cannot do so, as I am expecting Lord Pembroke to dinner."

"Will you be alone?"

"I expect so."

"I am glad to hear it; you will see my aunt and myself appearing on the scene."

"Here is my address; and I shall be delighted if you will come and see me."

She took the address, and I was surprised to see her smile as she read it.

"Then you are the Italian," she said, "who put up that notice that amused all the town?"

"I am."

"They say the joke cost you dear."

"Quite the reverse; it resulted in the greatest happiness."

"But now that the beloved object has left you, I suppose you are unhappy?"

"I am; but there are sorrows so sweet that they are almost joys."

"Nobody knows who she was, but I suppose you do?"

"Yes."

"Do you make a mystery of it?"

"Surely, and I would rather die than reveal it."

"Ask my aunt if I may take some rooms in your house; but I am afraid my mother would not let me."

"Why do you want to lodge cheaply?"

"I don't want to lodge cheaply, but I should like to punish the audacious author of that notice."

"How would you punish me?"

"By making you fall in love with me, and then tormenting you. It would have amused me immensely."

"Then you think that you can inspire me with love, and at the same time form the dreadful plan of tyrannising over the victim of your charms. Such a project is monstrous, and unhappily for us poor men, you do not look a monster. Nevertheless, I am obliged to you for your frankness, and I shall be on my guard."

"Then you must take care never to see me, or else all your efforts will be in vain."

As the Charpillon had laughed merrily through the whole of this dialogue, I took it all as a jest, but I could not help admiring her manner, which seemed made for the subjugation of men. But though I knew it not, the day I made that woman's acquaintance was a luckless one for me, as my readers will see.

It was towards the end of the month of September, 1763, when I met the Charpillon, and from that day I began to die. If the lines of ascent and declination are equal, now, on the first day of November, 1797, I have about four more years of life to reckon on, which will pass by swiftly, according to the axiom 'Motus in fine velocior'.

The Charpillon, who was well known in London, and I believe is still alive, was one of those beauties in whom it is difficult to find any positive fault. Her hair was chestnut coloured, and astonishingly long and thick, her blue eyes were at once languorous and brilliant, her skin, faintly tinged with a rosy hue, was of a dazzling whiteness; she was tall for her age, and seemed likely to become as tall as Pauline. Her breast was perhaps a little small, but perfectly shaped, her hands were white and plump, her feet small, and her gait had something noble and gracious. Her features were of that exquisite sensibility which gives so much charm to the fair sex, but nature had given her a beautiful body and a deformed soul. This siren had formed a design to wreck my happiness even before she knew me, and as if to add to her triumph she told me as much.

I left Malingan's house not like a man who, fond of the fair sex, is glad to have made the acquaintance of a beautiful woman, but in a state of stupefaction that the image of Pauline, which was always before me, was not strong enough to overcome the influence of a creature like the Charpillon, whom in my heart I could not help despising.

I calmed myself by saying that this strong impression was due to novelty, and by hoping that I should soon be disenchanted.

"She will have no charm," said I, "when I have once possessed her, and that will not be long in coming." Perhaps the reader will think that I was too presumptuous, but why should I suppose that there would be any difficulty? She had asked me to dinner herself, she had surrendered herself entirely to Morosini, who was not the man to sigh for long at any woman's feet, and must have paid her, for he was not young enough nor handsome enough to inspire her with a fancy for him. Without counting my physical attractions, I had plenty of money, and I was not afraid of spending it; and so I thought I could count on an easy victory.

Pembroke had become an intimate friend of mine since my proceedings with regard to Schwerin. He admired my conduct in not making any claim on the general for half my loss. He had said we would make a pleasant day of it together, and when he saw that my table was laid for four he asked who the other guests were to be. He was extremely surprised when he heard that they were the Charpillon and her aunt, and that the girl had invited herself when she heard he was to dine with me.

"I once took a violent fancy for the little hussy," said he. "It was one evening when I was at Vauxhall, and I offered her twenty guineas if she would come and take a little walk with me in a dark alley. She said she would come if I gave her the money in advance, which I was fool enough to do. She went with me, but as soon as we were alone she ran away, and I could not catch her again, though I looked for her all the evening."

"You ought to have boxed her ears before everybody."

"I should have got into trouble, and people would have laughed at me besides. I preferred to despise her and the money too. Are you in love with her?"

"No; but I am curious, as you were."

"Take care! she will do all in her power to entrap you."

She came in and went up to my lord with the most perfect coolness, and began to chatter away to him without taking any notice of me. She laughed, joked, and reproached him for not having pursued her at Vauxhall. Her stratagem, she said, was only meant to excite him the more.

"Another time," she added, "I shall not escape you."

"Perhaps not, my dear, for another time I shall take care not to pay in advance."

"Oh, fie! you degrade yourself by talking about paying."

"I suppose I honour you."

"We never talk of such things."

Lord Pembroke laughed at her impertinences, while she made a vigorous assault on him, for his coolness and indifference piqued her.

She left us soon after dinner, making me promise to dine with her the day after next.

I passed the next day with the amiable nobleman who initiated me into the mysteries of the English bagnio, an entertainment which I shall not describe, for it is well known to all who care to spend six guineas.

On the day appointed, my evil destiny made me go to the Charpillon's; the girl introduced me to her mother, whom I at once recollected, although she had aged and altered since I had seen her.

In the year 1759 a Genevan named Bolome had persuaded me to sell her jewels to the extent of six thousand francs, and she had paid me in bills drawn by her and her two sisters on this Bolome, but they were then known as Anspergher. The Genevan became bankrupt before the bills were due, and the three sisters disappeared. As may be imagined, I was surprised to find them in England, and especially to be introduced to them by the

Charpillon, who, knowing nothing of the affair of the jewels, had not told them that Seingalt was the same as Casanova, whom they had cheated of six thousand francs.

"I am delighted to see you again," were the first words I addressed to her.

"I recollect you, sir; that rascal Bolome . . . ."

"We will discuss that subject another time. I see you are ill."

"I have been at death's door, but I am better now. My daughter did not tell me your proper name."

"Yes, she did. My name is Seingalt as well as Casanova. I was known by the latter name at Paris when I made your daughter's acquaintance, though I did not know then that she was your daughter."

Just then the grandmother, whose name was also Anspergher, came in with the two aunts, and a quarter of an hour later three men arrived, one of whom was the Chevalier Goudar, whom I had met at Paris. I did not know the others who were introduced to me under the names of Rostaing and Caumon. They were three friends of the household, whose business it was to bring in dupes.

Such was the infamous company in which I found myself, and though I took its measure directly, yet I did not make my escape, nor did I resolve never to go to the house again. I was fascinated; I thought I would be on my guard and be safe, and as I only wanted the daughter I looked on all else as of little moment.

At table I led the conversation, and thought that my prey would soon be within my grasp. The only thing which annoyed me was that the Charpillon, after apologizing for having made me sit down to such a poor dinner, invited herself and all the company to sup with me on any day I liked to mention. I could make no opposition, so I begged her to name the day herself, and she did so, after a consultation with her worthy friends.

After coffee had been served we played four rubbers of whist, at which I lost, and at midnight I went away ill pleased with myself, but with no purpose of amendment, for this sorceress had got me in her toils.

All the same I had the strength of mind to refrain from seeing her for two days, and on the third, which was the day appointed for the cursed supper, she and her aunt paid me a call at nine o'clock in the morning.

"I have come to breakfast with you, and to discuss a certain question," said she, in the most engaging manner.

"Will you tell me your business now, or after breakfast?"

"After breakfast; for we must be alone."

We had our breakfast, and then the aunt went into another room, and the Charpillon, after describing the monetary situation of the family, told me that it would be much relieved if her aunt could obtain a hundred guineas.

"What would she do with the money?"

"She would make the Balm of Life, of which she possesses the secret, and no doubt she would make her fortune, too."

She then began to dilate on the marvellous properties of the balm, on its probable success in a town like London, and on the benefits which would accrue to myself, for of course I should share in the profits. She added that her mother and aunt would give me a written promise to repay the money in the course of six years.

"I will give you a decided answer after supper."

I then began to caress her, and to make assaults in the style of an amorous man, but it was all in vain, though I succeeded in stretching her on a large sofa. She made her escape, however, and ran to her aunt, while I followed her, feeling obliged to laugh as she did. She gave me her hand, and said,—

"Farewell, till this evening."

When they were gone, I reflected over what had passed and thought this first scene of no bad augury. I saw that I should get nothing out of her without spending a hundred guineas, and I determined not to attempt to bargain, but I would let her understand that she must make up her mind not to play prude. The game was in my hands, and all I had to do was to take care not to be duped.

In the evening the company arrived, and the girl asked me to hold a bank till supper was ready; but I declined, with a burst of laughter that seemed to puzzle her.

"At least, let us have a game of whist," said she.

"It seems to me," I answered, "that you don't feel very anxious to hear my reply."

"You have made up your mind, I suppose?"

"I have, follow me."

She followed me into an adjoining room, and after she had seated herself on a sofa, I told her that the hundred guineas were at her disposal.

"Then please to give the money to my aunt, otherwise these gentlemen might think I got it from you by some improper means."

"I will do so."

I tried to get possession of her, but in vain; and I ceased my endeavours when she said,—

"You will get nothing from me either by money or violence; but you can hope for all when I find you really nice and quiet."

I re-entered the drawing-room, and feeling my blood boiling I began to play to quiet myself. She was as gay as ever, but her gaiety tired me. At supper I had her on my right hand, but the hundred impertinences which, under other circumstances, would have amused me, only wearied me, after the two rebuffs I had received from her.

After supper, just as they were going, she took me aside, and told me that if I wanted to hand over the hundred guineas she would tell her aunt to go with me into the next room.

"As documents have to be executed," I replied, "it will take some time; we will talk of it again."

"Won't you fix the time?"

I drew out my purse full of gold, and shewed it her, saying,—

"The time depends entirely on you."

When my hateful guests were gone, I began to reflect, and came to the conclusion that this young adventuress had determined to plunder me without giving me anything in return. I determined to have nothing more to do with her, but I could not get her beauty out of my mind.

I felt I wanted some distraction, something that would give me new aims and make me forget her. With this idea I went to see my daughter, taking with me an immense bag of sweets.

As soon as I was in the midst of the little flock, the delight became general, Sophie distributing the sweetmeats to her friends, who received them gratefully.

I spent a happy day, and for a week or two I paid several visits to Harwich. The mistress treated me with the utmost politeness and my daughter with boundless affection, always calling me "dear papa."

In less than three weeks I congratulated myself on having forgotten the Charpillon, and on having replaced her by innocent amours, though one of my daughter's schoolmates pleased me rather too much for my peace of mind.

Such was my condition when one morning the favourite aunt of the Charpillon paid me a call, and said that they were all mystified at not having seen me since the supper I had given them, especially herself, as her niece had given her to understand that I would furnish her with the means of making the Balm of Life.

"Certainly; I would have given you the hundred guineas if your niece had treated me as a friend, but she refused me favours a vestal might have granted, and you must be aware that she is by no means a vestal."

"Don't mind my laughing. My niece is an innocent, giddy girl; she loves you, but she is afraid you have only a passing whim for her. She is in bed now with a bad cold, and if you will come and see her I am sure you will be satisfied."

These artful remarks, which had no doubt been prepared in advance, ought to have aroused all my scorn, but instead of that they awakened the most violent desires. I laughed in chorus with the old woman, and asked what would be the best time to call.

"Come now, and give one knock."

"Very good, then you may expect me shortly."

I congratulated myself on being on the verge of success, for after the explanation I had had with the aunt, and having, as I thought, a friend in her, I did not doubt that I should succeed.

I put on my great coat, and in less than a quarter of an hour I knocked at their door. The aunt opened to me, and said,—

"Come back in a quarter of an hour; she has been ordered a bath, and is just going to take it."

"This is another imposture. You're as bad a liar as she is."

"You are cruel and unjust, and if you will promise to be discreet, I will take you up to the third floor where she is bathing."

"Very good; take me." She went upstairs, I following on tiptoe, and pushed me into a room, and shut the door upon me. The Charpillon was in a huge bath, with her head towards the door, and the infernal coquette, pretending to think it was her aunt, did not move, and said,—

"Give me the towels, aunt."

She was in the most seductive posture, and I had the pleasure of gazing on her exquisite proportions, hardly veiled by the water.

When she caught sight of me, or rather pretended to do so, she gave a shriek, huddled her limbs together, and said, with affected anger,—

"Begone!"

"You needn't exert your voice, for I am not going to be duped."

"Begone!"

"Not so, give me a little time to collect myself."

"I tell you, go!"

"Calm yourself, and don't be afraid of my skewing you any violence; that would suit your game too well."

"My aunt shall pay dearly for this."

"She will find me her friend. I won't touch you, so shew me a little more of your charms."

"More of my charms?"

"Yes; put yourself as you were when I came in."

"Certainly not. Leave the room."

"I have told you I am not going, and that you need not fear for your . . . . well, for your virginity, we will say."

She then shewed me a picture more seductive than the first, and pretending kindliness, said,—

"Please, leave me; I will not fail to shew my gratitude."

Seeing that she got nothing, that I refrained from touching her, and that the fire she had kindled was in a fair way to be put out, she turned her back to me to give me to understand that it was no pleasure to her to look at me. However, my passions were running high, and I had to have recourse to self-abuse to calm my senses, and was glad to find myself relieved, as this proved to me that the desire went no deeper than the senses.

The aunt came in just as I had finished, and I went out without a word, well pleased to find myself despising a character wherein profit and loss usurped the place of feeling.

The aunt came to me as I was going out of the house, and after enquiring if I were satisfied begged me to come into the parlour.

"Yes," said I, "I am perfectly satisfied to know you and your niece. Here is the reward."

With these words I drew a bank-note for a hundred pounds from my pocket-book, and was foolish enough to give it her, telling her that she could make her balm, and need not trouble to give me any document as I knew if would be of no value. I had not the strength to go away without giving her anything, and the procuress was sharp enough to know it.

When I got home I reflected on what had happened, and pronounced myself the conqueror with great triumph. I felt well at ease, and felt sure that I should never set foot in that house again. There were seven of them altogether, including servants, and the need of subsisting made them do anything for a living; and when they found themselves obliged to make use of men, they summoned the three rascals I have named, who were equally dependent on them.

Five or six days afterwards, I met the little hussy at Vauxhall in company with Goudar. I avoided her at first, but she came up to me reproaching me for my rudeness. I replied coolly enough, but affecting not to notice my manner, she asked me to come into an arbour with her and take a cup of tea.

"No, thank you," I replied, "I prefer supper."

"Then I will take some too, and you will give it me, won't you, just to shew that you bear no malice?"

I ordered supper for four and we sat down together as if we had been intimate friends.

Her charming conversation combined with her beauty gradually drew me under her charm, and as the drink began to exercise its influence over me, I proposed a turn in one of the dark walks, expressing a hope that I should fare better than Lord Pembroke. She said gently, and with an appearance of sincerity that deceived me, that she wanted to be mine, but by day and on the condition that I would come and see her every day.

"I will do so, but first give me one little proof of your love."

"Most certainly not."

I got up to pay the bill, and then I left without a word, refusing to take her home. I went home by myself and went to bed.

The first thought when I awoke was that I was glad she had not taken me at my word; I felt very strongly that it was to my interest to break off all connection between that creature and myself. I felt the strength of her influence over me, and that my only way was to keep away from her, or to renounce all pretension to the possession of her charms.

The latter plan seemed to me impossible, so I determined to adhere to the first; but the wretched woman had resolved to defeat all my plans. The manner in which she succeeded must have been the result of a council of the whole society.

A few days after the Vauxhall supper Goudar called on me, and began by congratulating me on my resolution not to visit the Ansperghers any more, "for," said he, "the girl would have made you more and more in love with her, and in the end she would have seduced you to beggary."

"You must think me a great fool. If I had found her kind I should have been grateful, but without squandering all my money; and if she had been cruel, instead of ridiculous, I might have given her what I have already given her every day, without reducing myself to beggary."

"I congratulate you; it shews that you are well off. But have you made up your mind not to see her again?"

"Certainly."

"Then you are not in love with her?"

"I have been in love, but I am so no longer; and in a few days she will have passed completely out of my memory. I had almost forgotten her when I met her with you at Vauxhall."

"You are not cured. The way to be cured of an amour does not lie in flight, when the two parties live in the same town. Meetings will happen, and all the trouble has to be taken over again."

"Then do you know a better way?"

"Certainly; you should satiate yourself. It is quite possible that the creature is not in love with you, but you are rich and she has nothing. You might have had her for so much, and you could have left her when you found her to be unworthy of your constancy. You must know what kind of a woman she is."

"I should have tried this method gladly, but I found her out."

"You could have got the best of her, though, if you had gone to work in the proper way. You should never have paid in advance. I know everything."

"What do you mean?"

"I know she has cost you a hundred guineas, and that you have not won so much as a kiss from her. Why, my dear sir, you might have had her comfortably in your own bed for as much! She boasts that she took you in, though you pride yourself on your craft."

"It was an act of charity towards her aunt."

"Yes, to make her Balm of Life; but you know if it had not been for the niece the aunt would never have had the money."

"Perhaps not, but how come you who are of their party to be talking to me in this fashion?"

"I swear to you I only speak out of friendship for you, and I will tell you how I came to make the acquaintance of the girl, her mother, her grandmother and her two aunts, and then you will no longer consider me as of their party.

"Sixteen months ago I saw M. Morosini walking about Vauxhall by himself. He had just come to England to congratulate the king on his accession to the throne, on behalf of the Republic of Venice. I saw how enchanted he was with the London beauties, and I went up to him and told him that all these beauties were at his service. This made him laugh, and on my repeating that it was not a jest he pointed out one of the girls, and asked if she would be at his service. I did not know her, so I asked him to wait awhile, and I would bring him the information he required. There was no time to be lost, and I could see that the girl was not a vestal virgin, so I went up to her and told her that the Venetian ambassador was amorous of her, and that I would take her to him if she would receive his visits. The aunt said that a nobleman of such an exalted rank could only bring honour to her niece. I took their address, and on my way back to the ambassador I met a friend of mine who is learned in such commodities, and after I had shewed him the address he told me it was the Charpillon."

"And it was she?"

"It was. My friend told me she was a young Swiss girl who was not yet in the general market, but who would soon be there, as she was not rich, and had a numerous train to support.

"I rejoined the Venetian, and told him that his business was done, and asked him at what time I should introduce him the next day, warning him that as she had a mother and aunts she would not be alone.

"'I am glad to hear it,' said he, 'and also that she is not a common woman.' He gave me an appointment for the next day, and we parted.

"I told the ladies at what hour I should have the pleasure of introducing the great man to them, and after warning them that they must appear not to know him I went home.

"The following day I called on M. de Morosini, and took him to Denmark Street incognito. We spent an hour in conversation, and then went away without anything being settled. On the way back the ambassador told me that he should like to have the girl on conditions which he would give me in writing at his residence.

"These conditions were that she should live in a furnished house free of rent, without any companion, and without receiving any visitors. His excellency would give her fifty guineas a month, and pay for supper whenever he came and spent the night with her. He told me to get the house if his conditions were received. The mother was to sign the agreement.

"The ambassador was in a hurry, and in three days the agreement was signed; but I obtained a document from the mother promising to let me have the girl for one night as soon as the Venetian had gone; it was known he was only stopping in London for a year."

Goudar extracted the document in question from his pocket, and gave it to me. I read it and re-read it with as much surprise as pleasure, and he then proceeded with his story.

"When the ambassador had gone, the Charpillon, finding herself at liberty once more, had Lord Baltimore, Lord Grosvenor, and M. de Saa, the Portuguese ambassador, in turn, but no titular lover. I insisted on having my night with her according to agreement, but both mother and daughter laughed at me when I spoke of it. I cannot arrest her, because she is a minor, but I will have the mother imprisoned on the first opportunity, and you will see how the town will laugh. Now you know why I go to their house; and I assure you you are wrong if you think I have any part in their councils. Nevertheless, I know they are discussing how they may catch you, and they will do so if you do not take care."

"Tell the mother that I have another hundred guineas at her service if she will let me have her daughter for a single night."

"Do you mean that?"

"Assuredly, but I am not going to pay in advance."

"That's the only way not to be duped. I shall be glad to execute your commission."

I kept the rogue to dinner, thinking he might be useful to me. He knew everything and everybody, and told me a number of amusing anecdotes. Although a good-for-nothing fellow, he had his merits. He had written several works, which, though badly constructed, shewed he was a man of some wit. He was then writing his "Chinese Spy," and every day he wrote five or six news-letters from the various coffee-houses he frequented. I wrote one or two letters for him, with which he was much pleased. The reader will see how I met him again at Naples some years later.

The next morning, what was my surprise to see the Charpillon, who said with an air that I should have taken for modesty in any other woman,—

"I don't want you to give me any breakfast, I want an explanation, and to introduce Miss Lorenzi to you."

I bowed to her and to her companion, and then said,—

"What explanation do you require?"

At this, Miss Lorenzi, whom I had never seen before, thought proper to leave us, and I told my man that I was not at home to anybody. I ordered breakfast to be served to the companion of the nymph, that she might not find the waiting tedious.

"Sir," said the Charpillon, "is it a fact that you charged the Chevalier Goudar to tell my mother that you would give a hundred guineas to spend the night with me?"

"No, not to spend a night with you, but after I had passed it. Isn't the price enough?"

"No jesting, sir, if you please. There is no question of bargaining; all I want to know is whether you think you have a right to insult me, and that I am going to bear it?"

"If you think yourself insulted, I may, perhaps, confess I was wrong; but I confess I did not think I should have to listen to any reproaches from you. Gondar is one of your intimate friends, and this is not the first proposal he has taken to you. I could not address you directly, as I know your arts only too well."

"I shall not pay any attention to your abuse of my self; I will only remind you of what I said 'that neither money nor violence were of any use,' and that your only way was to make me in love with you by gentle means. Shew me where I have broken my word! It is you that have foresworn yourself in coming into my bath-room, and in sending such a brutal message to my mother. No one but a rascal like Goudar would have dared to take such a message."

"Goudar a rascal, is he? Well, he is your best friend. You know he is in love with you, and that he only got you for the ambassador in the hope of enjoying you himself. The document in his possession proves that you have behaved badly towards him. You are in his debt, discharge it, and then call him a rascal if you have the conscience to do so. You need not trouble to weep, for I knew the source of those tears; it is defiled."

"You know nothing of it. I love you, and it is hard to have you treat me so."

"You love me? You have not taken the best way to prove it!"

"As good a way as yours. You have behaved to me as if I were the vilest of prostitutes, and yesterday you seemed to think I was a brute beast, the slave of my mother. You should have written to me in person, and without the intervention of so vile an agent; I should have replied in the same way, and you need not have been afraid that you would be deceived."

"Supposing I had written, what would your answer have been?"

"I should have put all money matters out of question. I should have promised to content you on the condition that you would come and court me for a fortnight without demanding the slightest favour. We should have lived a pleasant life; we should have gone to the theatre and to the parks. I should have become madly in love with you. Then I should have given myself up to you for love, and nothing but love. I am ashamed to say that hitherto I have only given myself out of mere complaisance. Unhappy woman that I am! but I think nature meant me to love, and I thought when I saw you that my happy star had sent you to England that I might know the bliss of true affection. Instead of this you have only made me unhappy. You are the first man that has seen me weep; you have troubled my peace at home, for my mother shall never have the sum you promised her were it for nothing but a kiss."

"I am sorry to have injured you, though I did not intend to do so; but I really don't know what I can do."

"Come and see us, and keep your money, which I despise. If you love me, come and conquer me like a reasonable and not a brutal lover; and I will help you, for now you cannot doubt that I love you."

All this seemed so natural to me that I never dreamed it contained a trap. I was caught, and I promised to do what she wished, but only for a fortnight. She confirmed her promise, and her countenance became once more serene and calm. The Charpillon was a born actress.

She got up to go, and on my begging a kiss as a pledge of our reconciliation she replied, with a smile, the charm of which she well knew, that it would not do to begin by breaking the term of our agreement, and she left me more in love than ever, and full of repentance for my conduct.

# CHAPTER XII

Goudar's Chair

If she had written all this to me instead of coming and delivering it viva voce, it would probably have produced no effect; there would have been no tears, no ravishing features. She probably calculated all this, for women have a wonderful instinct in these matters.

That very evening I began my visits, and judged from my welcome that my triumph was nigh at hand. But love fills our minds with idle visions, and draws a veil over the truth.

The fortnight went by without my even kissing her hand, and every time I came I brought some expensive gift, which seemed cheap to me when I obtained such smiles of gratitude in exchange. Besides these presents, not a day passed without some excursion to the country or party at the theatre; that fortnight must have cost me four hundred guineas at the least.

At last it came to an end, and I asked her in the presence of her mother where she would spend the night with me, there or at my house. The mother said that we would settle it after supper, and I made no objection, not liking to tell her that in my house the supper would be more succulent, and a better prelude for the kind of exercise I expected to enjoy.

When we had supped the mother took me aside, and asked me to leave with the company and then to come back. I obeyed, laughing to myself at this foolish mystery, and when I came back I found the mother and the daughter in the parlour, in which a bed had been laid on the floor.

Though I did not much care for this arrangement, I was too amorous to raise any objection at a moment when I thought my triumph was at hand; but I was astonished when the mother asked me if I would like to pay the hundred guineas in advance.

"Oh, fie!" exclaimed the girl; and her mother left the room, and we locked the door.

My amorous feelings, so long pent up within my breast, would soon find relief. I approached her with open arms; but she avoided my caress, and gently begged me to get into bed while she prepared to follow me. I watched her undress with delight, but when she had finished she put out the candles. I complained of this act of hers, but she said she could not sleep with the light shining on her. I began to suspect that I might have some difficulties thrown in my way to sharpen the pleasure, but I determined to be resigned and to overcome them all.

When I felt her in the bed I tried to clasp her in my arms, but found that she had wrapped herself up in her long night-gown; her arms were crossed, and her head buried in her chest. I entreated, scolded, cursed, but all in vain; she let me go on, and answered not a word.

At first I thought it was a joke, but I soon found out my mistake; the veil fell from my eyes and I saw myself in my true colours, the degraded dupe of a vile prostitute.

Love easily becomes fury. I began to handle her roughly, but she resisted and did not speak. I tore her night-gown to rags, but I could not tear it entirely off her. My rage grew terrible, my hands became talons, and I treated her with the utmost cruelty; but all for nothing. At last, with my hand on her throat, I felt tempted to strangle her; and then I knew it was time for me to go.

It was a dreadful night. I spoke to this monster of a woman in every manner and tone-with gentleness, with argument, rage, remonstrance, prayers, tears, and abuse, but she resisted me for three hours without abandoning her painful position, in spite of the torments I made her endure.

At three o'clock in the morning, feeling my mind and body in a state of exhaustion, I got up and dressed myself by my sense of touch. I opened the parlour door, and finding the street door locked I shook it till a servant came and let me out. I went home and got into bed, but excited nature refused me the sleep I needed so. I took a cup of chocolate, but it would not stay on my stomach, and soon after a shivering fit warned me that I was feverish. I continued to be ill till the next day, and then the fever left me in a state of complete exhaustion.

As I was obliged to keep to my bed for a few days, I knew that I should soon get my health again; but my chief consolation was that at last I was cured. My shame had made me hate myself.

When I felt the fever coming on I told my man not to let anybody come to see me, and to place all my letters in my desk; for I wanted to be perfectly well before I troubled myself with anything.

On the fourth day I was better, and I told Jarbe to give me my letters. I found one from Pauline, dated from Madrid, in which she informed me that Clairmont had saved her life while they were fording a river, and she had determined to keep him till she got to Lisbon, and would then send him back by sea. I congratulated myself at the time on her resolve; but it was a fatal one for Clairmont, and indirectly for me also. Four months after, I heard that the ship in which he had sailed had been wrecked, and as I never heard from him again I could only conclude that my faithful servant had perished amidst the waves.

Amongst my London letters I found two from the infamous mother of the infamous Charpillon, and one from the girl herself. The first of the mother's letters, written before I was ill, told me that her daughter was ill in bed, covered with bruises from the blows I had given her, so that she would be obliged to institute legal proceedings against me. In the second letter she said she had heard I too was ill, and that she was sorry to hear it, her daughter having informed her that I had some reason for my anger; however, she would not fail to justify herself on the first opportunity. The Charpillon said in her letter that she knew she had done wrong, and that she wondered I had not killed her when I took her by the throat. She added that no doubt I had made up my mind to visit her no more, but she hoped I would allow her one interview as she had an important communication to make to me. There was also a note from Goudar, saying that he wanted to speak to me, and that he would come at noon. I gave orders that he should be admitted.

This curious individual began by astonishing me; he told me the whole story of what had taken place, the mother having been his informant.

"The Charpillon," he added, "has not got a fever, but is covered with bruises. What grieves the old woman most is that she has not got the hundred guineas."

"She would have had them the next morning," I said, "if her daughter had been tractable."

"Her mother had made her swear that she would not be tractable, and you need not hope to possess her without the mother's consent."

"Why won't she consent?"

"Because she thinks that you will abandon the girl as soon as you have enjoyed her."

"Possibly, but she would have received many valuable presents, and now she is abandoned and has nothing."

"Have you made up your mind not to have anything more to do with her?"

"Quite."

"That's your wisest plan, and I advise you to keep to it, nevertheless I want to shew you something which will surprise you. I will be back in a moment."

He returned, followed by a porter, who carried up an arm-chair covered with a cloth. As soon as we were alone, Goudar took off the covering and asked me if I would buy it.

"What should I do with it? It is not a very attractive piece of furniture."

"Nevertheless, the price of it is a hundred guineas."

"I would not give three."

"This arm-chair has five springs, which come into play all at once as soon as anyone sits down in it. Two springs catch the two arms and hold them tightly, two others separate the legs, and the fifth lifts up the seat."

After this description Goudar sat down quite naturally in the chair and the springs came into play and forced him into the position of a woman in labour.

"Get the fair Charpillon to sit in this chair," said he, "and your business is done."

I could not help laughing at the contrivance, which struck me as at once ingenious and diabolical, but I could not make up my mind to avail myself of it.

"I won't buy it," said I, "but I shall be obliged if you will leave it here till to-morrow."

"I can't leave it here an hour unless you will buy it; the owner is waiting close by to hear your answer."

"Then take it away and come back to dinner."

He shewed me how I was to release him from his ridiculous position, and then after covering it up again he called the porter and went away.

There could be no doubt as to the action of the machinery, and it was no feeling of avarice which hindered me from buying the chair. As I have said, it seemed rather a diabolical idea, and besides it might easily have sent me to the gallows. Furthermore, I should never have had the strength of mind to enjoy the Charpillon forcibly, especially by means of the wonderful chair, the mechanism of which would have frightened her out of her wits.

At dinner I told Goudar that the Charpillon had demanded an interview, and that I had wished to keep the chair so as to shew her that I could have her if I liked. I shewed him the letter, and he advised me to accede to her request, if only for curiosity's sake.

I was in no hurry to see the creature while the marks on her face and neck were still fresh, so I spent seven or eight days without making up my mind to receive her. Goudar came every day, and told me of the confabulations of these women who had made up their minds not to live save by trickery.

He told me that the grandmother had taken the name of Anspergher without having any right to it, as she was merely the mistress of a worthy citizen of Berne, by whom she had four daughters; the mother of the Charpillon was the youngest of the family, and, as she was pretty and loose in her morals, the Government had exiled her with her mother and sisters. They had then betaken themselves to Franche-Comté, where they lived for some time on the Balm of Life. Here it was that the Charpillon came into the world, her mother attributing her to a Count de Boulainvilliers. The child grew up pretty, and the family removed to Paris under the impression that it would be the best market for such a commodity, but in the course of four years the income from the Balm having dwindled greatly, the Charpillon being still too young to be profitable, and debtors closing round them on every side, they resolved to come to London.

He then proceeded to tell me of the various tricks and cheats which kept them all alive. I found his narrative interesting enough then, but the reader would find it dull, and I expect will be grateful for my passing it over.

I felt that it was fortunate for me that I had Goudar, who introduced me to all the most famous courtezans in London, above all to the illustrious Kitty Fisher, who was just beginning to be fashionable. He also introduced me to a girl of sixteen, a veritable prodigy of beauty, who served at the bar of a tavern at which we took a bottle of strong beer. She was an Irishwoman and a Catholic, and was named Sarah. I should have liked to get possession of her, but Goudar had views of his own on the subject, and carried her off in the course of the next year. He ended by marrying her, and she was the Sara Goudar who shone at Naples, Florence, Venice, and elsewhere. We shall hear of her in four or five years, still with her husband. Goudar had conceived the plan of making her take the place of Dubarry, mistress of Louis XV., but a lettre de cachet compelled him to try elsewhere. Ah! happy days of lettres de cachet, you have gone never to return!

The Charpillon waited a fortnight for me to reply, and then resolved to return to the charge in person. This was no doubt the result of a conference of the most secret kind, for I heard nothing of it from Gondar.

She came to see my by herself in a sedan-chair, and I decided on seeing her. I was taking my chocolate and I let her come in without rising or offering her any breakfast. She asked me to give her some with great modesty, and put up her face for me to give her a kiss, but I turned my head away. However, she was not in the least disconcerted.

"I suppose the marks of the blows you gave me make my face so repulsive?"

"You lie; I never struck you."

"No, but your tiger-like claws have left bruises all over me. Look here. No, you needn't be afraid that what you see may prove too seductive; besides, it will have no novelty for you."

So saying the wretched creature let me see her body, on which some livid marks were still visible.

Coward that I was! Why did I not look another way? I will tell you: it was because she was so beautiful, and because a woman's charms are unworthy of the name if they cannot silence reason. I affected only to look at the bruises, but it was an empty farce. I blush for myself; here was I conquered by a simple girl, ignorant of well nigh everything. But she knew well enough that I was inhaling the poison at every pore. All at once she dropped her clothes and came and sat beside me, feeling sure that I should have relished a continuance of the spectacle.

However, I made an effort and said, coldly, that it was all her own fault.

"I know it is," said she, "for if I had been tractable as I ought to have been, you would have been loving instead of cruel. But repentance effaces sin, and I am come to beg pardon. May I hope to obtain it?"

"Certainly; I am angry with you no longer, but I cannot forgive myself.
Now go, and trouble me no more."

"I will if you like, but there is something you have not heard, and I beg you will listen to me a moment."

"As I have nothing to do you can say what you have got to say, I will listen to you."

In spite of the coldness of my words, I was really profoundly touched, and the worst of it was that I began to believe in the genuineness of her motives.

She might have relieved herself of what she had to say in a quarter of an hour, but by dint of tears, sighs, groans, digressions, and so forth, she took two hours to tell me that her mother had made her swear to pass the night as she had done. She ended by saying that she would like to be mine as she had been M. Morosini's, to live with me, and only to go out under my escort, while I might allow her a monthly sum which she would hand over to her mother, who would, in that case, leave her alone.

She dined with me, and it was in the evening that she made this proposition. I suppose because she thought me ripe for another cheat. I told her that it might be arranged, but that I should prefer to settle with her mother, and that she would see me at their house the following day, and this seemed to surprise her.

It is possible that the Charpillon would have granted me any favour on that day, and then there would have been no question of deception or resistance for the future. Why did I not press her? Because sometimes love stupefies instead of quickens, and because I had been in a way her judge, and I thought it would be base of me to revenge myself on her by satisfying my amorous desires, and possibly because I was a fool, as I have often been in the course of my existence. She must have left me in a state of irritation, and no doubt she registered a vow to revenge herself on me for the half-contemptuous way in which I had treated her.

Goudar was astonished when he heard of her visit, and of the way in which I had spent the day. I begged him to get me a small furnished house, and in the evening I went to see the infamous woman in her own house.

She was with her mother, and I laid my proposal before them.

"Your daughter will have a house at Chelsea," said I to the mother, "where I can go and see her whenever I like, and also fifty guineas a month to do what she likes with."

"I don't care what you give her a month," she replied, "but before I let her leave my house she must give me the hundred guineas she was to have had when she slept with you."

"It is your fault that she didn't have them; however, to cut the matter short, she shall give them to you."

"And in the meanwhile, till you have found the house, I hope you will come and see me."

"Yes."

The next day Goudar shewed me a pretty house at Chelsea, and I took it, paying ten guineas, a month's rent, in advance, for which I received a receipt. In the afternoon I concluded the bargain with the mother, the Charpillon being present. The mother asked me to give her the hundred guineas, and I did so, not fearing any treachery, as nearly the whole of the girl's clothing was already at Chelsea.

In due course we went to our country house. The Charpillon liked the house immensely, and after a short talk we supped merrily together. After supper we went to bed, and she granted me some slight preliminary favours, but when I would have attained my end I found an obstacle which I had not expected. She gave me some physiological reasons for the circumstances, but not being a man to stop for so little, I would have gone on, but she resisted, and yet with such gentleness that I left her alone and went to sleep. I awoke sooner than she did, and determined to see whether she had imposed on me; so I raised her night-gown carefully, and took off her linen only to find that I had been duped once more. This roused her, and she tried to stop me, but it was too late. However, I gently chid her for the trick, and feeling disposed to forgive it set about making up for lost time, but she got on the high horse, and pretended to be hurt at my taking her by surprise. I tried to calm her by renewed tenderness, but the wretched creature only got more furious, and would give me nothing. I left her alone, but I expressed my opinion of her in pretty strong terms. The impudent slut honoured me with a smile of disdain, and then beginning to dress herself she proceeded to indulge in impertinent repartees. This made me angry, and I gave her a box on the ears which stretched her at full length on the floor. She shrieked, stamped her feet, and made a hideous uproar; the landlord came up, and she began to speak to him in English, while the blood gushed from her nose.

The man fortunately spoke Italian, and told me that she wanted to go away, and advised me to let her do so, or she might make it awkward for me, and he himself would be obliged to witness against me.

"Tell her to begone as fast as she likes," said I, "and to keep out of my sight for ever."

She finished dressing, staunched the blood, and went off in a sedan-chair, while I remained petrified, feeling that I did not deserve to live, and finding her conduct utterly outrageous and incomprehensible.

After an hour's consideration I decided on sending her back her trunk, and then I went home and to bed, telling my servants I was not at home to anyone.

I spent twenty-four hours in pondering over my wrongs, and at last my reason told me that the fault was mine; I despised myself. I was on the brink of suicide, but happily I escaped that fate.

I was just going out when Goudar came up and made me go in with him, as he said he wanted to speak to me. After telling me that the Charpillon had come home with a swollen cheek which prevented her shewing herself, he advised me to abandon all claims on her or her mother, or the latter would bring a false accusation against me which might cost me my life. Those who know England, and especially London will not need to be informed as to the nature of this accusation, which is so easily brought in England; it will suffice to say that through it Sodom was overwhelmed.

"The mother has engaged me to mediate," said Goudar, "and if you will leave her alone, she will do you no harm."

I spent the day with him, foolishly complaining, and telling him that he could assure the mother that I would take no proceedings against her, but that I should like to know if she had the courage to receive this assurance from my own lips.

"I will carry your message," said he, "but I pity you; for you are going into their nets again, and will end in utter ruin."

I fancied they would be ashamed to see me; but I was very much mistaken, for Goudar came back laughing, and said the mother expressed a hope that I should always be the friend of the family. I ought to have refused to have anything more to do with them, but I had not the strength to play the man. I called at Denmark Street the same evening, and spent an hour without uttering a syllable. The Charpillon sat opposite to me, with eyes lowered to a piece of embroidery, while from time to time she pretended to wipe away a tear as she let me see the ravages I had worked on her cheek.

I saw her every day and always in silence till the fatal mark had disappeared, but during these mad visits the poison of desire was so instilled into my veins that if she had known my state of mind she might have despoiled me of all I possessed for a single favour.

When she was once more as beautiful as ever I felt as if I must die if I did not hold her in my arms again, and I bought a magnificent pier-glass and a splendid breakfast service in Dresden china, and sent them to her with an amorous epistle which must have made her think me either the most extravagant or the most cowardly of men. She wrote in answer that she would expect me to sup with her in her room, that she might give me the tenderest proofs of her gratitude.

This letter sent me completely mad with joy, and in a paroxysm of delight
I resolved to surrender to her keeping the two bills of exchange which
Bolomee had given me, and which gave me power to send her mother and
aunts to prison.

Full of the happiness that awaited me, and enchanted with my own idiotic heroism, I went to her in the evening. She received me in the parlour with her mother, and I was delighted to see the pier-glass over the mantel, and the china displayed on a little table. After a hundred words of love and tenderness she asked me to come up to her room, and her mother wished us good night. I was overwhelmed with joy. After a delicate little supper I took out the bills of exchange, and after telling her their history gave them up to her, to shew that I had no intention of avenging myself on her mother and aunts. I made her promise that she would never part with them, and she said she would never do so, and with many expressions of gratitude and wonder at my generosity she locked them up with great care.

Then I thought it was time to give her some marks of my passion, and I found her kind; but when I would have plucked the fruit, she clasped me to her arms, crossed her legs, and began to weep bitterly.

I made an effort, and asked her if she would be the same when we were in bed. She sighed, and after a moment's pause, replied, "Yes."

For a quarter of an hour I remained silent and motionless, as if petrified. At last I rose with apparent coolness, and took my cloak and sword.

"What!" said she, "are you not going to spend the night with me?"

"No."

"But we shall see each other to-morrow?"

"I hope so. Good night."

I left that infernal abode, and went home to bed.

## CHAPTER XIII

The End of the Story Stranger Than the Beginning

At eight o'clock the next morning Jarbe told me that the Charpillon wanted to see me, and that she had sent away her chairmen.

"Tell her that I can't see her."

But I had hardly spoken when she came in, and Jarbe went out. I addressed her with the utmost calmness, and begged her to give me back the two bills of exchange I had placed in her hands the night before.

"I haven't got them about me; but why do you want me to return them to you?"

At this question I could contain myself no longer, and launched a storm of abuse at her. It was an explosion which relieved nature, and ended with an involuntary shower of tears. My infamous seductress stood as calmly as Innocence itself; and when I was so choked with sobs that I could not utter a word, she said she had only been cruel because her mother had made her swear an oath never to give herself to anyone in her own house, and that she had only come now to convince me of her love, to give herself to me without reserve, and never to leave me any more if I wished it.

The reader who imagines that at these words rage gave place to love, and that I hastened to obtain the prize, does not know the nature of the passion so well as the vile woman whose plaything I was. From hot love to hot anger is a short journey, but the return is slow and difficult. If there be only anger in a man's breast it may be subdued by tenderness, by submission, and affection; but when to anger is added a feeling of indignation at having been shamefully deceived, it is impossible to pass suddenly to thoughts of love and voluptuous enjoyment. With me mere anger has never been of long duration, but when I am indignant the only cure is forgetfulness.

The Charpillon knew perfectly well that I would not take her at her word, and this kind of science was inborn in her. The instinct of women teaches them greater secrets than all the philosophy and the research of men.

In the evening this monster left me, feigning to be disappointed and disconsolate, and saying,—

"I hope you will come and see me again when you are once more yourself."

She had spent eight hours with me, during which time she had only spoken to deny my suppositions, which were perfectly true, but which she could not afford to let pass. I had not taken anything all day, in order that I might not be obliged to offer her anything or to eat with her.

After she had left me I took some soup and then enjoyed a quiet sleep, for which I felt all the better. When I came to consider what had passed the day before I concluded that the Charpillon was repentant, but I seemed no longer to care anything about her.

Here I may as well confess, in all humility, what a change love worked on me in London, though I had attained the age of thirty-eight. Here closed the first act of my life; the second closed when I left Venice in 1783, and probably the third will close here, as I amuse myself by writing these memoirs. Thus, the three-act comedy will finish, and if it be hissed, as may possibly be the case, I shall not hear the sounds of disapproval. But as yet the reader has not seen the last and I think the most interesting scene of the first act.

I went for a walk in the Green Park and met Goudar. I was glad to see him, as the rogue was useful to me.

"I have just been at the Charpillons," he began; "they were all in high spirits. I tried in vain to turn the conversation on you, but not a word would they utter."

"I despise them entirely," I rejoined, "I don't want to have anything more to do with them."

He told me I was quite right, and advised me to persevere in my plan. I made him dine with me, and then we went to see the well-known procuress, Mrs. Wells, and saw the celebrated courtezan, Kitty Fisher, who was waiting for the Duke of—— to take her to a ball. She was magnificently dressed, and it is no exaggeration to say that she had on diamonds worth five hundred thousand francs. Goudar told me that if I liked I might have her then and there for ten guineas. I did not care to do so, however, for, though charming, she could only speak English, and I liked to have all my senses, including that of hearing, gratified. When she had gone, Mrs. Wells told us that Kitty had eaten a bank-note for a thousand guineas, on a slice of bread and butter, that very day.

The note was a present from Sir Akins, brother of the fair Mrs. Pitt. I do not know whether the bank thanked Kitty for the present she had made it.

I spent an hour with a girl named Kennedy, a fair Irishwoman, who could speak a sort of French, and behaved most extravagantly under the influence of champagne; but the image of the Charpillon was still before me, though I knew it not, and I could not enjoy anything. I went home feeling sad and ill pleased with myself. Common sense told me to drive all thoughts of that wretched woman out of my head, but something I called honour bade me not leave her the triumph of having won the two bills of exchange from me for nothing, and made me determine to get them back by fair means or foul.

M. Malingan, at whose house I had made the acquaintance of this creature, come and asked me to dinner. He had asked me to dine with him several times before, and I had always refused, and now I would not accept until I had heard what guests he had invited. The names were all strange to me, so I agreed to come.

When I arrived I found two young ladies from Liege, in one of whom I got interested directly. She introduced me to her husband, and to another young man who seemed to be the cavalier of the other lady, her cousin.

The company pleased me, and I was in hopes that I should spend a happy day, but my evil genius brought the Charpillon to mar the feast. She came into the room in high glee, and said to Malingan,—

"I should not have come to beg you to give me a dinner if I had known that you would have so many guests, and if I am at all in the way I will go."

Everybody welcomed her, myself excepted, for I was on the rack. To make matters worse, she was placed at my left hand. If she had come in before we sat down to dinner I should have made some excuse and gone away, but as we had begun the soup a sudden flight would have covered me with ridicule. I adopted the plan of not looking at her, reserving all my politeness for the lady on my right. When the meal was over Malingan took me apart, and swore to me that he had not invited the Charpillon, but I was not convinced, though I pretended to be for politeness' sake.

The two ladies from Liege and their cavaliers were embarking for Ostend in a few days, and in speaking of their departure the one to whom I had taken a fancy said that she was sorry to be leaving England without having seen Richmond. I begged her to give me the pleasure of shewing it her, and without waiting for an answer I asked her husband and all the company to be present, excepting the Charpillon, whom I pretended not to see.

The invitation was accepted.

"Two carriages," I said, "holding four each, shall be ready at eight o'clock, and we shall be exactly eight."

"No, nine, for I am coming," said the Charpillon, giving me an impudent stare, "and I hope you will not drive me away."

"No, that would be impolite, I will ride in front on horseback."

"Oh, not at all! Emilie shall sit on my lap."

Emilie was Malingan's daughter, and as everybody seemed to think the arrangement an extremely pleasant one I had not the courage to resist. A few moments after, I was obliged to leave the room for a few moments, and when I came back I met her on the landing. She told me I had insulted her grievously, and that unless I made amends I should feel her vengeance.

"You can begin your vengeance," I said, "by returning my bills of exchange."

"You shall have them to-morrow, but you had better try and make me forget the insult you have put on me."

I left the company in the evening, having arranged that we should all breakfast together the next day.

At eight o'clock the two carriages were ready, and Malingan, his wife, his daughter, and the two gentlemen got into the first vehicle, and I had to get into the second with the ladies from Liege and the Charpillon, who seemed to have become very intimate with them. This made me ill-tempered, and I sulked the whole way. We were an hour and a quarter on the journey, and when we arrived I ordered a good dinner, and then we proceeded to view the gardens; the day was a beautiful one, though it was autumn.

Whilst we were walking the Charpillon came up to me and said she wanted to return the bills in the same place in which I had given her them. As we were at some distance from the others I pelted her with abuse, telling her of her perfidy and of her corruption at an age when she should have retained some vestiges of innocence calling her by the name she deserved, as I reminded her how often she had already prostituted herself; in short I threatened her with my vengeance if she pushed me to extremities. But she was as cold as ice, and opposed a calm front to the storm of invective I rained in her ears. However, as the other guests were at no great distance, she begged me to speak more softly, but they heard me and I was very glad of it.

At last we sat down to dinner, and the wretched woman contrived to get a place beside me, and behaved all the while as if I were her lover, or at any rate as if she loved me. She did not seem to care what people thought of my coldness, while I was in a rage, for the company must either have thought me a fool or else that she was making game of me.

After dinner we returned to the garden, and the Charpillon, determined to gain the victory, clung to my arm and after several turns led me towards the maze where she wished to try her power. She made me sit down on the grass beside her and attacked me with passionate words and tender caresses, and by displaying the most interesting of her charms she succeeded in seducing me, but still I do not know whether I were impelled by love or vengeance, and I am inclined to think that my feelings were a compound of both passions.

But at the moment she looked the picture of voluptuous abandon. Her ardent eyes, her fiery cheeks, her wanton kisses, her swelling breast, and her quick sighs, all made me think that she stood as much in need of defeat as I of victory; certainly I should not have judged that she was already calculating on resistance.

Thus I once more became tender and affectionate; I begged pardon for what I had said and done. Her fiery kisses replied to mine, and I thought her glance and the soft pressure of her body were inviting me to gather the delicious fruit; but just as my hand opened the door of the sanctuary, she gave a sudden movement, and the chance was lost.

"What! you would deceive me again."

"No, no but we have done enough now. I promise to spend the night in your arms in your own house."

For a moment I lost my senses. I only saw the deceitful wretch who had profited by my foolish credulity so many times, and I resolved to enjoy or take vengeance. I held her down with my left arm, and drawing a small knife from my pocket I opened it with my teeth and pricked her neck, threatening to kill her if she resisted me.

"Do as you like," she said with perfect calm, "I only ask you to leave me my life, but after you have satisfied yourself I will not leave the spot; I will not enter your carriage unless you carry me by force, and everybody shall know the reason."

This threat had no effect, for I had already got back my senses, and I pitied myself for being degraded by a creature for whom I had the greatest contempt, in spite of the almost magical influence she had over me, and the furious desires she knew how to kindle in my breast. I rose without a word, and taking my hat and cane I hastened to leave a place where unbridled passion had brought me to the brink of ruin.

My readers will scarcely believe me (but it is nevertheless the exact truth) when I say that the impudent creature hastened to rejoin me, and took my arm again as if nothing had happened. A girl of her age could not have played the part so well unless she had been already tried in a hundred battles. When we rejoined the company I was asked if I were ill, while nobody noticed the slightest alteration in her.

When we got back to London I excused myself under the plea of a bad headache, and returned home.

The adventure had made a terrible impression on me, and I saw that if I did not avoid all intercourse with this girl I should be brought to ruin. There was something about her I could not resist. I therefore resolved to see her no more, but feeling ashamed of my weakness in giving her the bills of exchange I wrote her mother a note requesting her to make her daughter return them, or else I should be compelled to take harsh measures.

In the afternoon I received the following reply:

"Sir,—I am exceedingly surprised at your addressing yourself to me about the bills you handed to my daughter. She tells me she will give you them back in person when you shew more discretion, and have learnt to respect her."

This impudent letter so enraged me that I forgot my vow of the morning. I put two pistols in my pocket and proceeded to the wretched woman's abode to compel her to return me my bills if she did not wish to be soundly caned.

I only took the pistols to overawe the two male rascals who supped with them every evening. I was furious when I arrived, but I passed by the door when I saw a handsome young hairdresser, who did the Charpillon's hair every Saturday evening, going into the house.

I did not want a stranger to be present at the scene I meant to make, so I waited at the corner of the street for the hairdresser to go. After I had waited half an hour Rostaing and Couman, the two supports of the house, came out and went away, much to my delight. I waited on; eleven struck, and the handsome barber had not yet gone. A little before midnight a servant came out with a lamp, I suppose to look for something that had fallen out of the window. I approached noiselessly, stepped in and opened the parlour-door, which was close to the street, and saw . . . the Charpillon and the barber stretched on the sofa and doing the beast with two backs, as Shakespeare calls it.

When the slut saw me she gave a shriek and unhorsed her gallant, whom I caned soundly until he escaped in the confusion consequent on the servants, mother, and aunts all rushing into the room. While this was going on the Charpillon, half-naked, remained crouched behind the sofa, trembling lest the blows should begin to descend on her. Then the three hags set upon me like furies; but their abuse only irritated me, and I broke the pier-

'glass, the china, and the furniture, and as they still howled and shrieked I roared out that if they did not cease I would break their heads. At this they began to calm.

I threw myself upon the fatal sofa, and bade the mother to return me the bills of exchange; but just then the watchman came in.

There is only one watchman to a district, which he perambulates all night with a lantern in one hand and a staff in the other. On these men the peace of the great city depends. I put three or four crowns into his hand and said "Go away," and so saying shut the door upon him. Then I sat down once more and asked again for the bills of exchange:

"I have not got them; my daughter keeps them."

"Call her."

The two maids said that whilst I was breaking the china she had escaped by the street door, and that they did not know what had become of her. Then the mother and aunts began to shriek, weep, and exclaim,—

"My poor daughter alone in the streets of London at midnight! My dear niece, alas! alas! she is lost. Cursed be the hour when you came to England to make us all unhappy!"

My rage had evaporated, and I trembled at the thought of this young frightened girl running about the streets at such an hour.

"Go and look for her at the neighbours' houses," I said to the servants, "no doubt you will find her. When you tell me she is safe, you shall have a guinea apiece."

When the three Gorgons saw I was interested, their tears, complaints, and invectives began again with renewed vigor, while I kept silence as much as to say that they were in the right. I awaited the return of the servants with impatience, and at last at one o'clock they came back with looks of despair.

"We have looked for her everywhere," said they, "but we can't find her."

I gave them the two guineas as if they had succeeded, whilst I sat motionless reflecting on the terrible consequences of my anger. How foolish is man when he is in love!

I was idiot enough to express my repentance to the three old cheats. I begged them to seek for her everywhere when dawn appeared, and to let me know of her return that I might fall at her feet to beg pardon, and never see her face again. I also promised to pay for all the damage I had done, and to give them a full receipt for the bills of exchange. After these acts, done to the everlasting shame of my good sense, after this apology made to procuresses who laughed at me and my honour, I went home, promising two guineas to the servant who should bring me tidings that her young mistress had come home. On leaving the house I found the watchman at the door; he had been waiting to see me home. It was two o'clock. I threw myself on my bed, and the six hours of sleep I obtained, though troubled by fearful dreams, probably saved me from madness.

At eight o'clock I heard a knock at the door, and on opening the window found it was one of the servants from the house of my foes. I cried out to let her in, and I breathed again on hearing that Miss Charpillon had just arrived in a sedan-chair in a pitiable condition, and that she had been put to bed.

"I made haste to come and tell you," said the cunning maid, "not for the sake of your two guineas, but because I saw you were so unhappy." This duped me directly. I gave her the two guineas, and made her sit down on my bed, begging her to tell me all about her mistress's return. I did not dream that she had been schooled by my enemies; but during the whole of this period I was deprived of the right use of my reason.

The slut began by saying that her young mistress loved me, and had only deceived me in accordance with her mother's orders.

"I know that," I said, "but where did she pass the night?"

"At a shop which she found open, and where she was known from having bought various articles there. She is in bed with a fever, and I am afraid it may have serious consequences as she is in her monthly period."

"That's impossible, for I caught her in the act with her hairdresser."

"Oh, that proves nothing! the poor young man does not look into things very closely."

"But she is in love with him."

"I don't think so, though she has spent several hours in his company."

"And you say that she loves me!"

"Oh, that has nothing to do with it! It is only a whim of hers with the hairdresser."

"Tell her that I am coming to pass the day beside her bed, and bring me her reply."

"I will send the other girl if you like."

"No, she only speaks English."

She went away, and as she had not returned by three o'clock I decided on calling to hear how she was. I knocked at the door, and one of the aunts appeared and begged me not to enter as the two friends of the house were there in a fury against me, and her niece lay in a delirium, crying out "There's Seingalt, there's Seingalt! He's going to kill me. Help! help!" "For God's sake, sir, go away!"

I went home desperate, without the slightest suspicion that it was all a lie. I spent the whole day without eating anything; I could not swallow a mouthful. All night I kept awake, and though I took several glasses of strong waters I could obtain no rest.

At nine o'clock the next morning I knocked at the Charpillon's door, and the old aunt came and held it half open as before. She forbade me to enter, saying that her niece was still delirious, continually calling on me in her transports, and that the doctor had declared that if the disease continued its course she had not twenty-four hours to live. "The fright you gave her has arrested her periods; she is in a terrible state."

"O, fatal hairdresser!" I exclaimed.

"That was a mere youthful folly; you should have pretended not to have seen anything."

"You think that possible, you old witch, do you? Do not let her lack for anything; take that."

With these words I gave her a bank note for ten guineas and went away, like the fool I was. On my way back I met Goudar, who was quite frightened at my aspect. I begged him to go and see how the Charpillon really was, and then to come and pass the rest of the day with me. An hour after he came back and said he had found them all in tears and that the girl was in extremis.

"Did you see her?"

"No, they said she could see no one."

"Do you think it is all true?"

"I don't know what to think; but one of the maids, who tells me the truth as a rule, assured me that she had become mad through her courses being stopped, while she has also a fever and violent convulsions. It is all credible enough, for these are the usual results of a shock when a woman is in such a situation. The girl told me it was all your fault."

I then told him the whole story. He could only pity me, but when he heard that I had neither eaten nor slept for the last forty-eight hours he said very wisely that if I did not take care I should lose my reason or my life. I knew it, but I could find no remedy. He spent the day with me and did me good. As I could not eat I drank a good deal, and not being able to sleep I spent the night in striding up and down my room like a man beside himself.

On the third day, having heard nothing positive about the Charpillon, I went out at seven o'clock in the morning to call on her. After I had waited a quarter of an hour in the street, the door was partly opened, and I saw the mother all in tears, but she would not let me come in. She said her daughter was in the last agony. At the same instant a pale and thin old man came out, telling the mother that we must resign ourselves to the will of God. I asked the infamous creature if it were the doctor.

"The doctor is no good now," said the old hypocrite, weeping anew, "he is a minister of the Gospel, and there is another of them upstairs. My poor daughter! In another hour she will be no more."

I felt as if an icy hand had closed upon my heart. I burst into tears and left the woman, saying,—

"It is true that my hand dealt the blow, but her death lies at your door."

As I walked away my knees seemed to bend under me, and I entered my house determined to commit suicide,—

With this fearful idea, I gave orders that I was not at home to anyone. As soon as I got to my room I put my watches, rings, snuff-boxes, purse and pocket-book in my casket, and shut it up in my escritoire. I then wrote a letter to the Venetian ambassador, informing him that all my property was to go to M. de Bragadin after my death. I sealed the letter and put it with the casket, and took the key with me, and also silver to the amount of a few guineas. I took my pistols and went out with the firm intention of drowning myself in the Thames, near the Tower of London.

Pondering over my plan with the utmost coolness, I went and bought some balls of lead as large as my pockets would hold, and as heavy as I could bear, to carry to the Tower, where I intended to go on foot. On my way I was strengthened in my purpose by the reflection, that if I continued to live I should be tormented for the remainder of my days by the pale shade of the Charpillon reproaching me as her murderer. I even congratulated myself on being able to carry out my purpose without any effort, and I also felt a secret pride in my courage.

I walked slowly on account of the enormous weight I bore, which would assure me a speedy passage to the bottom of the river.

By Westminster Bridge my good fortune made me meet Sir Edgar, a rich young Englishman, who lived a careless and joyous life. I had made his acquaintance at Lord Pembroke's, and he had dined with me several times. We suited one another, his conversation was agreeable, and we had passed many pleasant hours together. I tried to avoid him, but he saw me, and came up and took me by the arm in a friendly manner.

"Where are you going? Come with me, unless you are going to deliver some captive. Come along, we shall have a pleasant party."

"I can't come, my dear fellow, let me go."

"What's the matter? I hardly recognized you, you looked so solemn."

"Nothing is the matter."

"Nothing? You should look at your face in the glass. Now I feel quite sure that you are going to commit a foolish action."

"Not at all."

"It's no good denying it."

"I tell you there's nothing the matter with me. Good bye, I shall see you again."

"It's no good, I won't leave you. Come along, we will walk together."

His eyes happening to fall on my breeches pocket, he noticed my pistol, and putting his hand on the other pocket he felt the other pistol, and said,—

"You are going to fight a duel; I should like to see it. I won't interfere with the affair, but neither will I leave you."

I tried to put on a smile, and assured him that he was mistaken, and that I was only going for a walk to pass the time.

"Very good," said Edgar, "then I hope my society is as pleasant to you as yours is to me; I won't leave you. After we have taken a walk we will go and dine at the 'Canon.' I will get two girls to come and join us, and we shall have a gay little party of four."

"My dear friend, you must excuse me; I am in a melancholy mood, and I want to be alone to get over it."

"You can be alone to-morrow, if you like, but I am sure you will be all right in the next three hours, and if not, why I will share your madness. Where did you think of dining?"

"Nowhere; I have no appetite. I have been fasting for the last three days, and I can only drink."

"Ah! I begin to see daylight. Something has crossed you, and you are going to let it kill you as it killed one of my brothers. I must see what can be done."

Edgar argued, insisted, and joked till at last I said to myself, "A day longer will not matter, I can do the deed when he leaves me, and I shall only have to bear with life a few hours longer."

When Edgar heard that I had no particular object in crossing the bridge he said that we had better turn back, and I let myself be persuaded; but in half an hour I begged him to take me somewhere where I could wait for him, as I could not bear the weight of the lead any longer. I gave him my word of honour that I would meet him at the "Canon."

As soon as I was alone I emptied my pockets, and put the leaden balls into a cupboard. Then I lay down and began to consider whether the good-natured young man would prevent me committing suicide, as he had already made me postpone it.

I reasoned, not as one that hopes, but rather as one that foresaw that Edgar would hinder me from shortening my days. Thus I waited in the tavern for the young Englishman, doubtful whether he was doing me a service or an injury.

He came back before long, and was pleased to find me.

"I reckoned on your keeping your word," said he.

"You did not think that I would break my word of honour."

"That's all right; I see you are on the way to recovery."

The sensible and cheerful talk of the young man did me good, and I began to feel better, when the two young wantons, one of whom was a Frenchwoman, arrived in high spirits. They seemed intended for pleasure, and Nature had dowered them with great attractions. I appreciated their charms, but I could not welcome them in the manner to which they were accustomed. They began to think me some poor valetudinarian; but though I was in torments, a feeling of vanity made me endeavour to behave sensibly. I gave them some cold kisses and begged Edgar to tell his fellow-countrywoman that if I were not three parts dead I would prove how lovely and charming I thought her. They pitied me. A man who has spent three days without eating or sleeping is almost incapable of any voluptuous excitement, but mere words would not have convinced these priestesses of Venus if Edgar had not given them my name. I had a reputation, and I saw that when they heard who I was they were full of respect. They all hoped that Bacchus and Comus would plead the cause of Love, and I let them talk, knowing that their hopes were vain.

We had an English dinner; that is, a dinner without the essential course of soup, so I only took a few oysters and a draught of delicious wine, but I felt better, and was pleased to see Edgar amusing himself with the two nymphs.

The young madcap suddenly proposed that the girls should dance a hornpipe in the costume of Mother Eve, and they consented on the condition that we would adopt the dress of Father Adam, and that blind musicians were summoned. I told them that I would take off my clothes to oblige them, but that I had no hopes of being able to imitate the seductive serpent. I was allowed to retain my dress, on the condition that if I felt the prick of the flesh I should immediately undress. I agreed to do so, and the blind musicians were sent for, and while they tuned their instruments toilettes were made, and the orgy began.

It taught me same useful lessons. I learnt from it that amorous pleasures are the effect and not the cause of gaiety. I sat gazing at three naked bodies of perfect grace and beauty, the dance and the music were ravishing and seductive, but nothing made any impression on me. After the dance was over the male dancer treated the two females, one after the other, until he was forced to rest. The French girl came up to ascertain whether I skewed any signs of life, but feeling my hopeless condition she pronounced me useless.

When it was all over I begged Edgar to give the French girl four guineas, and to pay my share, as I had very little money about me.

What should I have said if I had been told in the morning that instead of drowning myself I should take part in so pleasant an entertainment?

The debt I had contracted with the young Englishman made me resolve to put off my suicide to another day. After the nymphs had gone I tried to get rid of Edgar, but in vain; he told me I was getting better, that the oysters I had taken skewed my stomach was improving, and that if I came with him to Ranelagh I should be able to make a good dinner the next day. I was weak and indifferent and let myself be persuaded, and got into a coach with Edgar in obedience to the Stoic maxim I had learnt in the happy days of my youth: 'Sequere Deum'.

We entered the fine rotunda with our hats off, and began to walk round and round, our arms behind our backs—a common custom in England, at least in those days.

A minuet was being danced, and I was so attracted by a lady who danced extremely well that I waited for her to turn round. What made me notice her more particularly was that her dress and hat were exactly like those I had given to the Charpillon a few days before, but as I believed the poor wretch to be dead or dying the likeness did not inspire me with any suspicion. But the lady turned round, lifted her face, and I saw—the Charpillon herself!

Edgar told me afterwards that at that moment he thought to see me fall to the ground in an epileptic fit; I trembled and shuddered so terribly.

However, I felt so sure she was ill that I could not believe my own eyes, and the doubt brought me to my senses.

"She can't be the Charpillon," I said to myself, "she is some other girl like her, and my enfeebled senses have led me astray." In the meanwhile the lady, intent on her dancing, did not glance in my direction, but I could afford to wait. At last she lifted her arms to make the curtsy at the end of the minuet, I went up instinctively as if I were about to dance with her; she looked me in the face, and fled.

I constrained myself; but now that there could be no doubt my shuddering fit returned, and I made haste to sit down. A cold sweat bedewed my face and my whole body. Edgar advised me to take a cup of tea but I begged him to leave me alone for a few moments.

I was afraid that I was on the point of death; I trembled all over, and my heart beat so rapidly that I could not have stood up had I wished.

At last, instead of dying, I got new life. What a wonderful change I experienced! Little by little my peace of mind returned, and I could enjoy the glitter of the multitudinous wax lights. By slow degrees I passed through all the shades of feeling between despair and an ecstasy of joy. My soul and mind were so astonished by the shock that I began to think I should never see Edgar again.

"This young man," I said to myself, "is my good genius, my guardian angel, my familiar spirit, who has taken the form of Edgar to restore me to my senses again."

I should certainly have persisted in this idea if my friend had not reappeared before very long.

Chance might have thrown him in the way of one of those seductive creatures who make one forget everything else; he might have left Ranelagh without having time to tell me he was going, and I should have gone back to London feeling perfectly certain that I had only seen his earthly shape. Should I have been disabused if I had seen him a few days after? Possibly; but I am not sure of it. I have always had a hankering after superstition, of which I do not boast; but I confess the fact, and leave the reader to judge me.

However, he came back in high spirits, but anxious about me. He was surprised to find me full of animation, and to hear me talking in a pleasant strain on the surrounding objects and persons.

"Why, you are laughing!" said he, "your sadness has departed, then?"

"Yes, good genius, but I am hungry, and I want you to do me a favour, if you have no other pressing engagements."

"I am free till the day after to-morrow, and till then you can do what you like with me."

"I owe my life to you, but to make your gift complete I want you to spend this night and the whole of the next day with me."

"Done."

"Then let us go home."

"With all my heart; come along."

I did not tell him anything as we were in the coach, and when we got home I found nothing fresh, except a note from Goudar, which I put in my pocket, intending to reserve all business for the next day.

It was an hour after midnight. A good supper was served to us, and we fell to; for my part I devoured my food like a wild beast. Edgar congratulated me, and we went to bed, and I slept profoundly till noon. When I awoke I breakfasted with Edgar, and told him the whole story, which would have ended with my life if he had not met me on Westminster Bridge, and he had not been keen enough to mark my condition. I took him to my room, and shewed him my escritoire, my casket, and my will. I then opened Goudar's letter, and read:

"I am quite sure that the girl you know of is very far from dying, as she has gone to Ranelagh with Lord Grosvenor."

Although Edgar was a profligate, he was a sensible man, and my story made him furious. He threw his arms around my neck, and told me he should always think the day on which he rescued me from death for so unworthy an object the happiest in his life. He could scarcely credit the infamy of the Charpillon and her mother.

He told me I could have the mother arrested, though I had not got the bills of exchange, as her mother's letter acknowledging her daughter's possession of the bills was sufficient evidence.

Without informing him of my intention, I resolved that moment to have her arrested. Before we parted we swore eternal friendship, but the reader will see before long what a penance the kind Englishman had to do for befriending me.

The next day I went to the attorney I had employed against Count Schwerin. After hearing my story he said that I had an undoubted claim, and that I could arrest the mother and the two aunts.

Without losing time I went before a magistrate, who took my sworn information and granted me a warrant. The same official who had arrested Schwerin took charge of the affair; but as he did not know the women by sight it was necessary that someone who did should go with him, for though he was certain of surprising them there might be several other women present, and he might not arrest the right ones.

As Goudar would not have undertaken the delicate task of pointing them out, I resolved on accompanying him myself.

I made an appointment with him at an hour when I knew they would be all in the parlour. He was to enter directly the door was opened, and I would come in at the same instant and point out the women he had to arrest. In England all judicial proceedings are conducted with the utmost punctuality, and everything went off as I had arranged. The bailiff and his subaltern stepped into the parlour and I followed in their footsteps. I pointed out the mother and the two sisters and then made haste to escape, for the sight of the Charpillon, dressed in black, standing by the hearth, made me shudder. I felt cured, certainly; but the wounds she had given me were not yet healed, and I cannot say what might have happened if the Circe had had the presence of mind to throw her arms about my neck and beg for mercy.

As soon as I had seen these women in the hands of justice I fled, tasting the sweets of vengeance, which are very great, but yet a sign of unhappiness. The rage in which I had arrested the three procuresses, and my terror in seeing the woman who had well-nigh killed me, shewed that I was not really cured. To be so I must fly from them and forget them altogether.

The next morning Goudar came and congratulated me on the bold step I had taken, which proved, he said, that I was either cured or more in love than ever. "I have just come from Denmark Street," he added, "and I only saw the grandmother, who was weeping bitterly, and an attorney, whom no doubt she was consulting."

"Then you have heard what has happened?"

"Yes, I came up a minute after you had gone and I stayed till the three old sluts made up their minds to go with the constable. They resisted and said he ought to leave them till the next day, when they would be able to find someone to bail them. The two bravos drew their swords to resist the law, but the other constable disarmed them one after the other, and the three women were led off. The Charpillon wanted to accompany them, but it was judged best that she should remain at liberty, in order to try and set them free."

Goudar concluded by saying that he should go and see them in prison, and if I felt disposed to come to an arrangement he would mediate between us. I told him that the only arrangement I would accept was the payment of the six thousand francs, and that they might think themselves very lucky that I did not insist on having my interest, and thus repaying myself in part for the sums they had cheated out of me.

A fortnight elapsed without my hearing any more of the matter. The Charpillon dined with them every day, and in fact, kept them. It must have cost her a good deal, for they had two rooms, and their landlord would not allow them to have their meals prepared outside the prison. Goudar told me that the Charpillon said she would never beg me to listen to her mother, though she knew she had only to call on me to obtain anything she wanted. She thought me the most abominable of men. If I feel obliged to maintain that she was equally abominable, I must confess that on this occasion she shewed more strength of mind than I; but whereas I had acted out of passion, her misdeeds were calculated, and tended solely to her own interests.

For the whole of this fortnight I had sought for Edgar in vain, but one morning he came to see me, looking in high spirits.

"Where have you been hiding all this time?" said I, "I have been looking for you everywhere."

"Love has been keeping me a prisoner," said he, "I have got some money for you."

"For me? From what quarter?"

"On behalf of the Ansperghers. Give me a receipt and the necessary declaration, for I am going to restore them myself to the poor Charpillon, who has been weeping for the last fortnight."

"I daresay she has, I have seen her weep myself; but I like the way in which she has chosen the being who delivered me from her chains as a protector. Does she know that I owe my life to you?"

"She only knew that I was with you at Ranelagh when you saw her dancing instead of dying, but I have told her the whole story since."

"No doubt she wants you to plead with me in her favour."

"By no means. She has just been telling me that you are a monster of ingratitude, for she loved you and gave you several proofs of her affection, but now she hates you."

"Thank Heaven for that! The wretched woman! It's curious she should have selected you as her lover by way of taking vengeance on me, but take care! she will punish you."

"It may be so, but at all events it's a pleasant kind of punishment."

"I hope you may be happy, but look to yourself; she is a mistress in all sorts of deceit."

Edgar counted me out two hundred and fifty guineas, for which I gave him a receipt and the declaration he required, and with these documents he went off in high spirits.

After this I might surely flatter myself that all was at an end between us, but I was mistaken.

Just about this time the Crown Prince of Brunswick, now the reigning duke, married the King of England's sister. The Common Council presented him with the freedom of the City, and the Goldsmith's Company admitted him into their society, and gave him a splendid box containing the documents which made him a London citizen. The prince was the first gentleman in Europe, and yet he did not disdain to add this new honour to a family illustrious for fourteen hundred years.

On this occasion Lady Harrington was the means of getting Madame Cornelis two hundred guineas. She lent her room in Soho Square to a confectioner who gave a ball and supper to a thousand persons at three guineas each. I paid my three guineas, and had the honour of standing up all the evening with six hundred others, for the table only seated four hundred, and there were several ladies who were unable to procure seats. That evening I saw Lady Grafton seated beside the Duke of Cumberland. She wore her hair without any powder, and all the other ladies were exclaiming about it, and saying how very unbecoming it was. They could not anathematize the innovator too much, but in less than six months Lady Grafton's style of doing the hair became common, crossed the Channel, and spread all over Europe, though it has been given another name. It is still in fashion, and is the only method that can boast the age of thirty years, though it was so unmercifully ridiculed at first.

The supper for which the giver of the feast had received three thousand guineas, or sixty-five thousand francs, contained a most varied assortment of delicacies, but as I had not been dancing, and did not feel taken with any of the ladies present, I left at one in the morning. It was Sunday, a day on which all persons, save criminals, are exempt from arrest; but, nevertheless, the following adventure befell me:

I was dressed magnificently, and was driving home in my carriage, with my negro and another servant seated behind me; and just as we entered Pall Mall I heard a voice crying, "Good night, Seingalt." I put my head out of the window to reply, and in an instant the carriage was surrounded by men armed with pistols, and one of them said,—

"In the king's name!"

My servant asked what they wanted, and they answered,—

"To take him to Newgate, for Sunday makes no difference to criminals."

"And what crime have I committed?"

"You will hear that in prison."

"My master has a right to know his crime before he goes to prison," said the negro.

"Yes, but the magistrate's abed."

The negro stuck to his position, however, and the people who had come up declared with one consent that he was in the right.

The head-constable gave in, and said he would take me to a house in the city.

"Then drive to that city," said I, "and have done with it."

We stopped before the house, and I was placed in a large room on the ground floor, furnished solely with benches and long tables. My servant sent back the carriage, and came to keep me company. The six constables said they could not leave me, and told me I should send out for some meat and drink for them. I told my negro to give them what they wanted, and to be as amicable with them as was possible.

As I had not committed any crime, I was quite at ease; I knew that my arrest must be the effect of a slander, and as I was aware that London justice was speedy and equitable, I thought I should soon be free. But I blamed myself for having transgressed the excellent maxim, never to answer anyone in the night time; for if I had not done so I should have been in my house, and not in prison. The mistake, however, had been committed, and there was nothing to be done but to wait patiently. I amused myself by reflecting on my rapid passage from a numerous and exalted assemblage to the vile place I now occupied, though I was still dressed like a prince.

At last the day dawned, and the keeper of the tavern came to see who the prisoner was. I could not helping laughing at him when he saw me, for he immediately began to abuse the constables for not awaking him when I came; he had lost the guinea I should have paid for a private room. At last news was brought that the magistrate was sitting, and that I must be brought up.

A coach was summoned, and I got into it, for if I had dared to walk along the streets in my magnificent attire the mob would have pelted me.

I went into the hall of justice, and all eyes were at once attracted towards me; my silks and satins appeared to them the height of impertinence.

At the end of the room I saw a gentleman sitting in an arm-chair, and concluded him to be my judge. I was right, and the judge was blind. He wore a broad band round his head, passing over his eyes. A man beside me, guessing I was a foreigner, said in French,—

"Be of good courage, Mr. Fielding is a just and equitable magistrate."

I thanked the kindly unknown, and was delighted to see before me this famous and estimable writer, whose works are an honour to the English nation.

When my turn came, the clerk of the court told Mr. Fielding my name, at least, so I presume.

"Signor Casanova," said he, in excellent Italian, "be kind enough to step forward. I wish to speak to you."

I was delighted to hear the accents of my native tongue, and making my way through the press I came up to the bar of the court, and said,—

"Eccomi, Signore."

He continued to speak Italian, and said,—

"Signor de Casanova, of Venice, you are condemned to perpetual confinement in the prisons of His Majesty the King of Great Britain."

"I should like to know, sir, for what crime I am condemned. Would you be kind enough to inform me as to its nature?"

"Your demand is a reasonable one, for with us no one is condemned without knowing the cause of his condemnation. You must know, then, that the accusation (which is supported by two witnesses) charges you with intending to do grievous bodily harm to the person of a pretty girl; and as this pretty girl aforesaid goes in dread of you, the law decrees that you must be kept in prison for the rest of your days."

"Sir, this accusation is a groundless calumny; to that I will take my oath! It is very possible indeed that the girl may fear my vengeance when she comes to consider her own conduct, but I can assure you that I have had no such designs hitherto, and I don't think I ever shall."

"She has two witnesses."

"Then they are false ones. But may I ask your worship the name of my accuser?"

"Miss Charpillon."

"I thought as much; but I have never given her aught but proofs of my affection."

"Then you have no wish to do her any bodily harm?"

"Certainly not."

"Then I congratulate you. You can dine at home; but you must find two sureties. I must have an assurance from the mouths of two householders that you will never commit such a crime."

"Whom shall I find to do so?"

"Two well-known Englishmen, whose friendship you have gained, and who know that you are incapable of such an action. Send for them, and if they arrive before I go to dinner I will set you at liberty."

The constable took me back to prison, where I had passed the night, and I gave my servants the addresses of all the householders I recollected, bidding them explain my situation, and to be as quick as possible. They ought to have come before noon, but London is such a large place! They did not arrive, and the magistrate went to dinner. I comforted myself by the thought that he would sit in the afternoon, but I had to put up with a disagreeable experience.

The chief constable, accompanied by an interpreter, came to say that I must go to Newgate. This is a prison where the most wretched and abject criminals are kept.

I signified to him that I was awaiting bail, and that he could take me to Newgate in the evening if it did not come, but he only turned a deaf ear to my petition. The interpreter told me in a whisper that the fellow was certainly paid by the other side to put me to trouble, but that if I liked to bribe him I could stay where I was.

"How much will he want?"

The interpreter took the constable aside, and then told me that I could stay where I was for ten guineas.

"Then say that I should like to see Newgate."

A coach was summoned, and I was taken away.

When I got to this abode of misery and despair, a hell, such as Dante might have conceived, a crowd of wretches, some of whom were to be hanged in the course of the week, greeted me by deriding my elegant attire. I did not answer them, and they began to get angry and to abuse me. The gaoler quieted them by saying that I was a foreigner and did not understand English, and then took me to a cell, informing me how much it would cost me, and of the prison rules, as if he felt certain that I should make a long stay. But in the course of half an hour, the constable who had tried to get ten guineas out of me told me that bail had arrived and that my carriage was at the door.

I thanked God from the bottom of my heart, and soon found myself in the presence of the blind magistrate. My bail consisted of Pegu, my tailor, and Maisonneuve, my wine merchant, who said they were happy to be able to render me this slight service. In another part of the court I noticed the infamous Charpillon, Rostaing, Goudar, and an attorney. They made no impression on me, and I contented myself with giving them a look of profound contempt.

My two sureties were informed of the amount in which they were to bail me, and signed with a light heart, and then the magistrate said, politely,—

"Signor Casanova, please to sign your name for double the amount, and you will then be a free man again."

I went towards the clerk's table, and on asking the sum I was to answer for was informed that it was forty guineas, each of my sureties signing for twenty. I signed my name, telling Goudar that if the magistrate could have seen the Charpillon he would have valued her beauty at ten thousand guineas. I asked the names of the two witnesses, and was told that they were Rostaing and Bottarelli. I looked contemptuously at Rostaing, who was as pale as death, and averting my face from the Charpillon out of pity, I said,—

"The witnesses are worthy of the charge."

I saluted the judge with respect, although he could not see me, and asked the clerk if I had anything to pay. He replied in the negative, and a dispute ensued between him and the attorney of my fair enemy, who was disgusted on hearing that she could not leave the court without paying the costs of my arrest.

Just as I was going, five or six well-known Englishmen appeared to bail me out, and were mortified to hear that they had come too late. They begged me to forgive the laws of the land, which are only too often converted into a means for the annoyance of foreigners.

At last, after one of the most tedious days I have ever spent, I returned home and went to bed, laughing at the experience I had undergone.

# The End